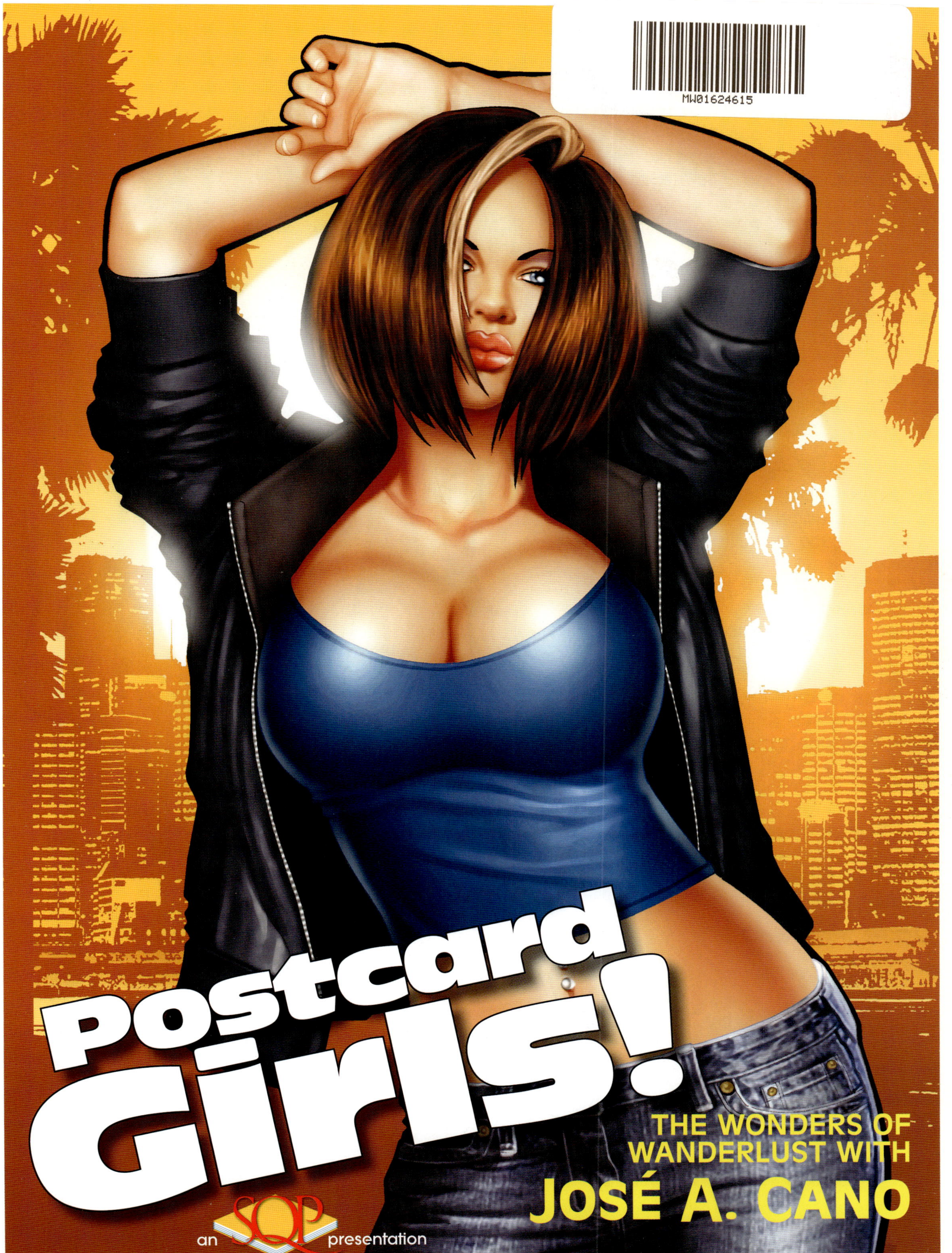
Postcard
Girls!
THE WONDERS OF
WANDERLUST WITH
JOSÉ A. CANO
an SQP presentation

Travel can be so expanding...

As an artist, I'm pretty much a prisoner to my drawing table. Most of my time (okay, ALL of my time) is spent illustrating beautiful women. Don't feel too bad - It's a sacrifice I willingly make for my art.
When I create these sultry portraits of such lovely ladies, my imagination is as important to the process as my brush. As I render every line, caress every curve, and color ever delicious bounce and bump, I let my mind wander and begin to fantasize.
Hey - they're MY illustrations!
When I put together this collection of paintings, they began to resemble a gallery of snapshots from perhaps the greatest road-trip I'd never been on! Since I was the ultimate creator of these drawings, I decided to be their ultimate travelling companion as well.
With this in mind, I present *"Postcard Girls" Volume One* - an illustrated thought experiment/every guy's fantasy committed to paper.
Did I have fun? Oh yes! Did I have to spend an untold fortune in airline tickets, hotel rooms and expensive dinners? No!
I hope you enjoy these precious portraits as much as I enjoyed "sight-seeing" with them!
Wishing you were here!

José A. Cano

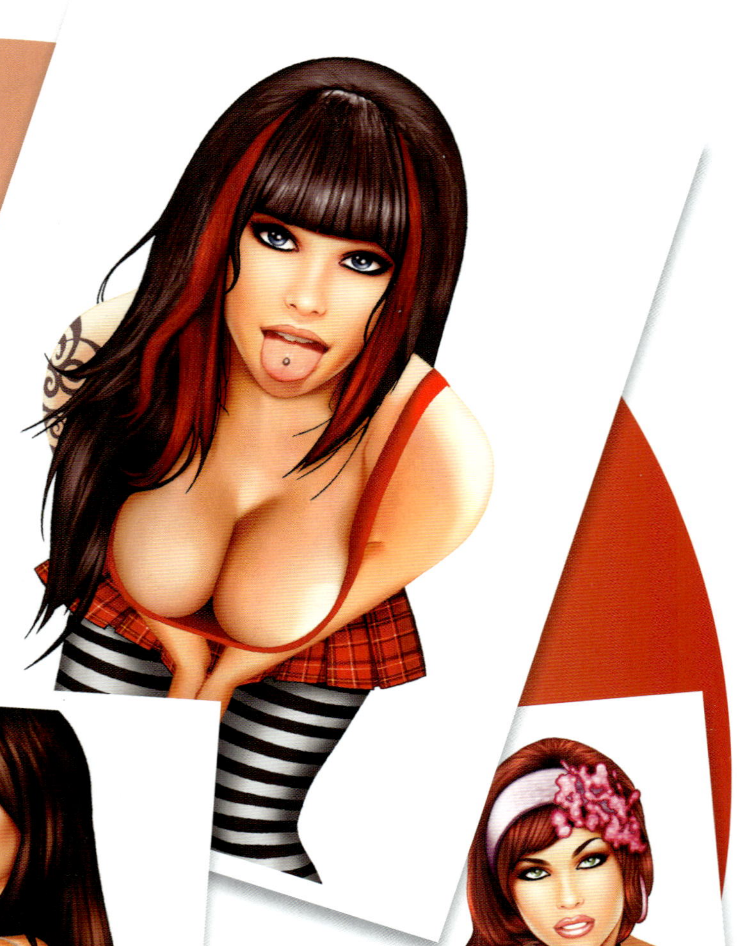

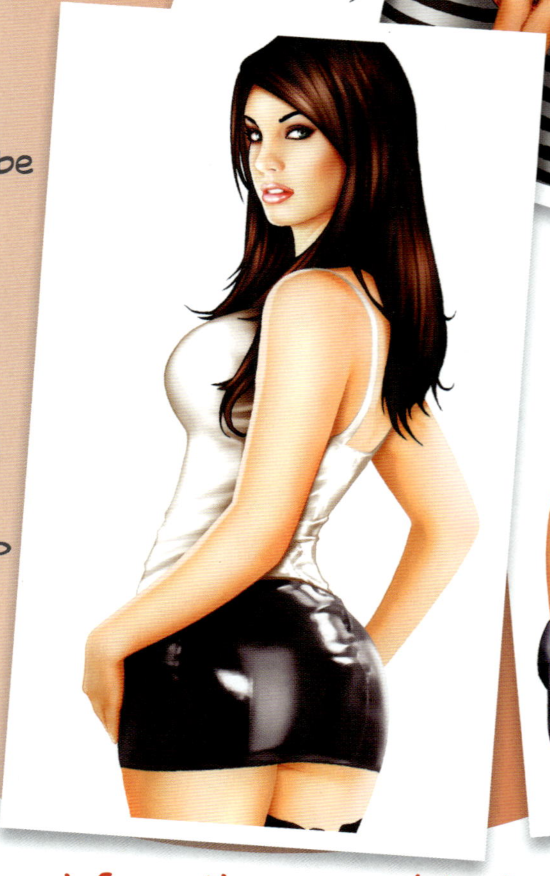

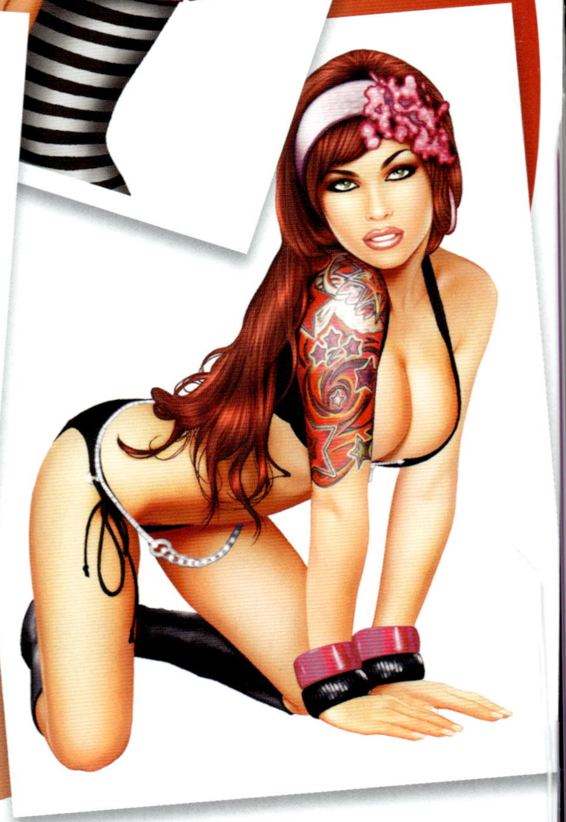

For news, updates, and more information on my latest work, go to: www.canoart.net

Postcard Girls! by José A. Cano

Book design by Grassy Knoll Studios.

Published by SQP Inc.
PO Box 248 - Columbus NJ 08022

Sal Quartuccio & Bob Keenan - Publishers

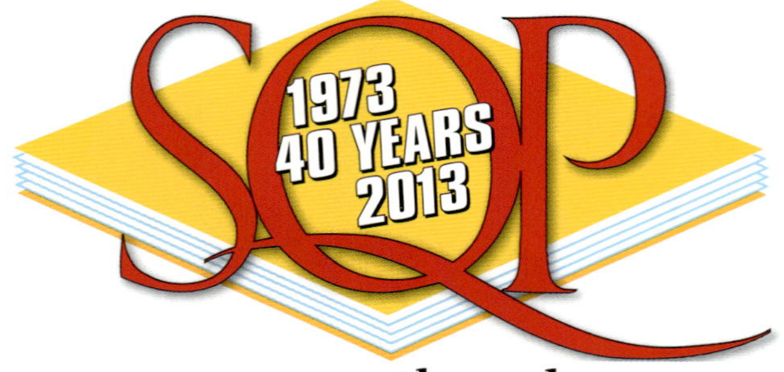

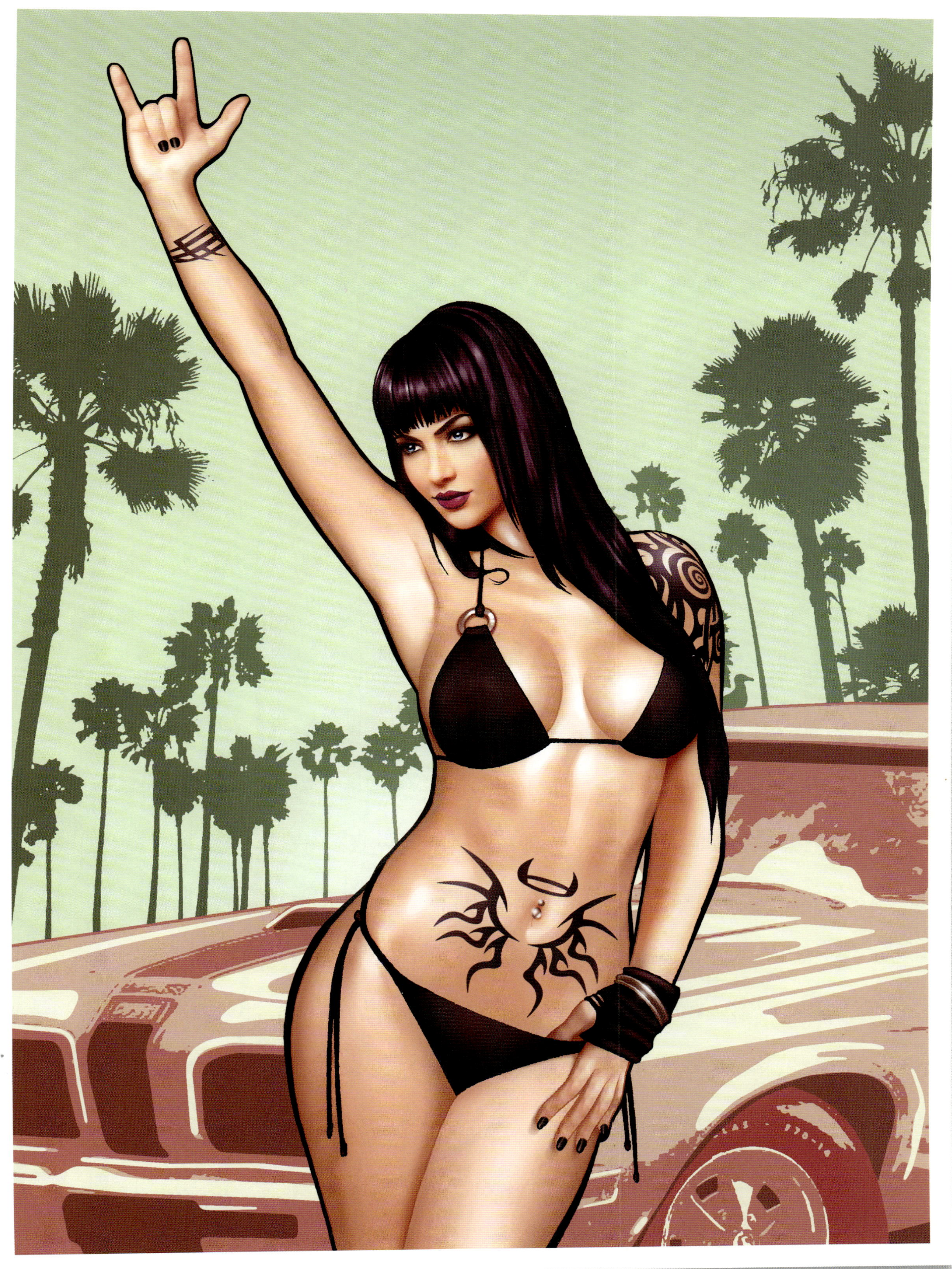

Cassandra rocked the beach and made the day even hotter!

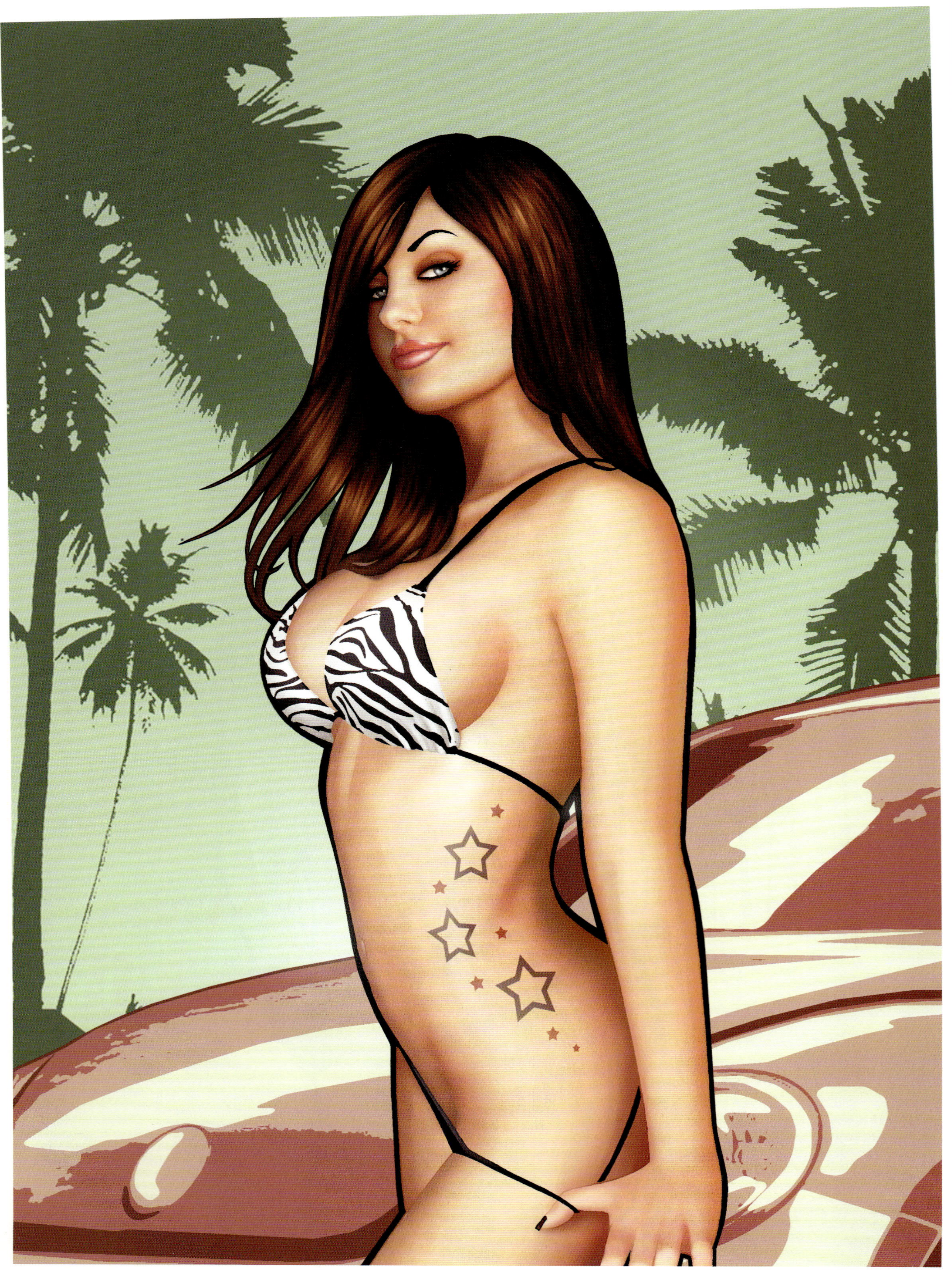

Pull a thread, see what unravels!

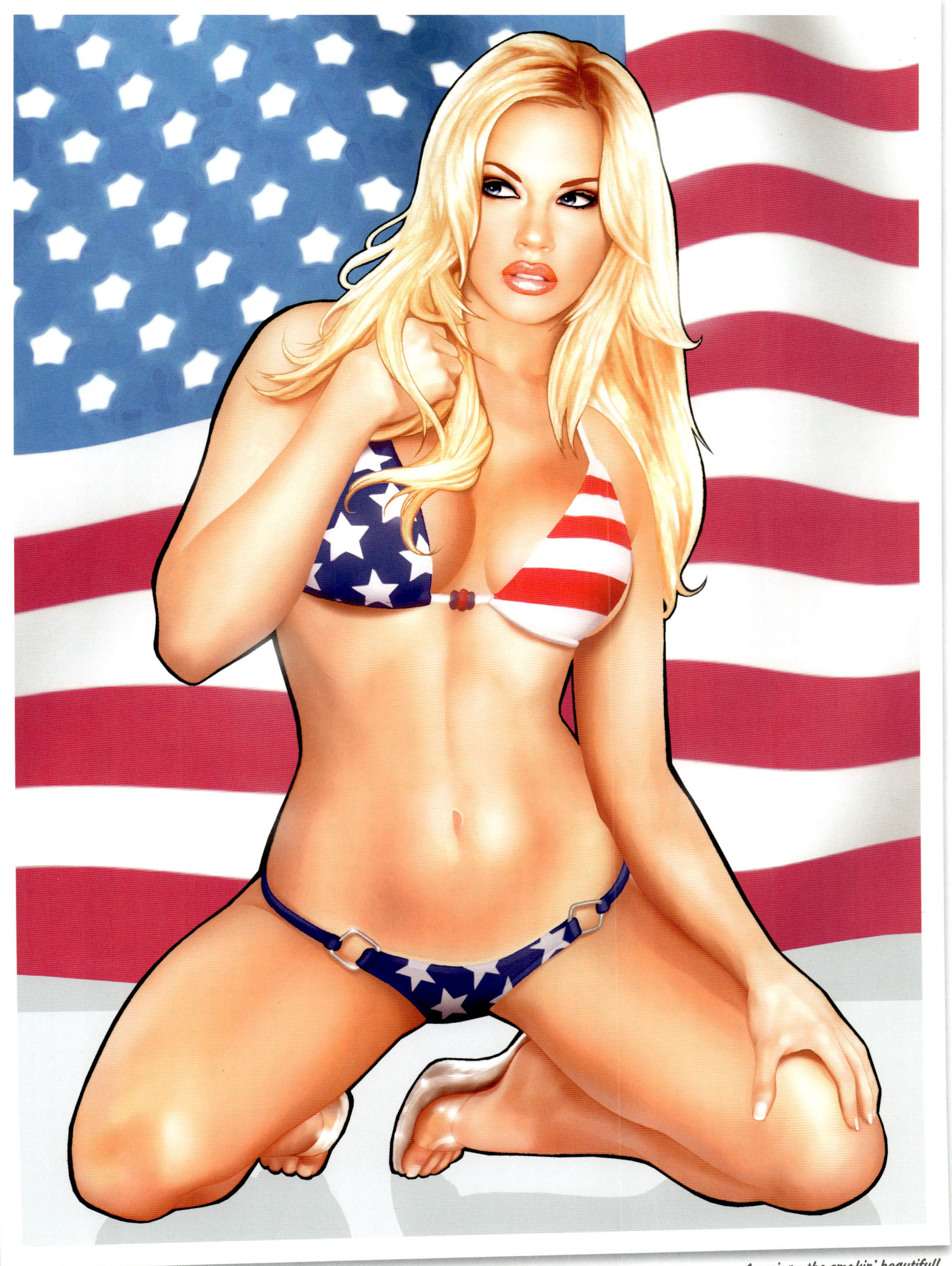

America - the smokin' beautiful!

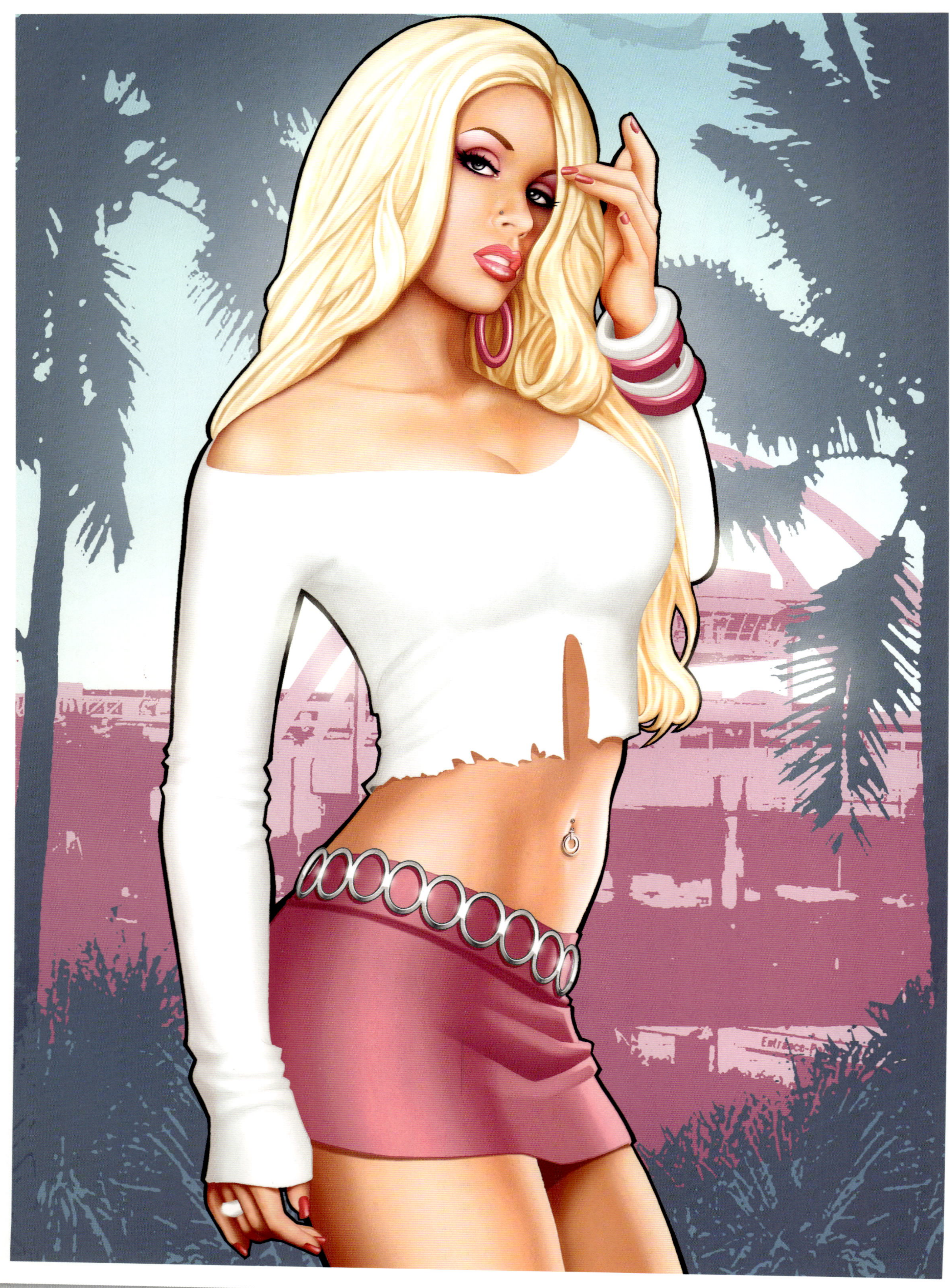

Picked up a FOX at LAX. More "X"s to follow?

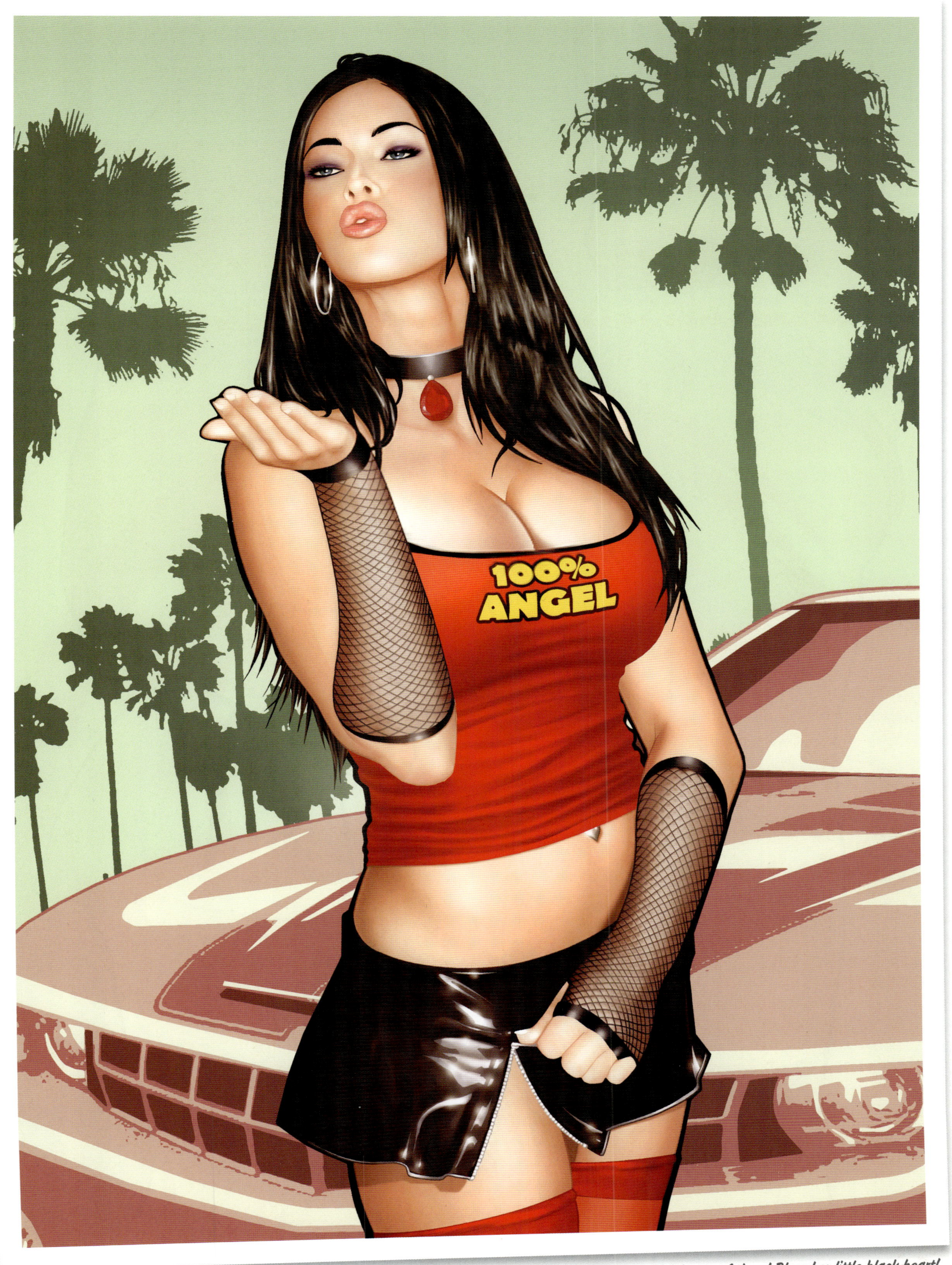

Roxy is a lot of things - "100% Angel" ain't one of them! Bless her little black heart!

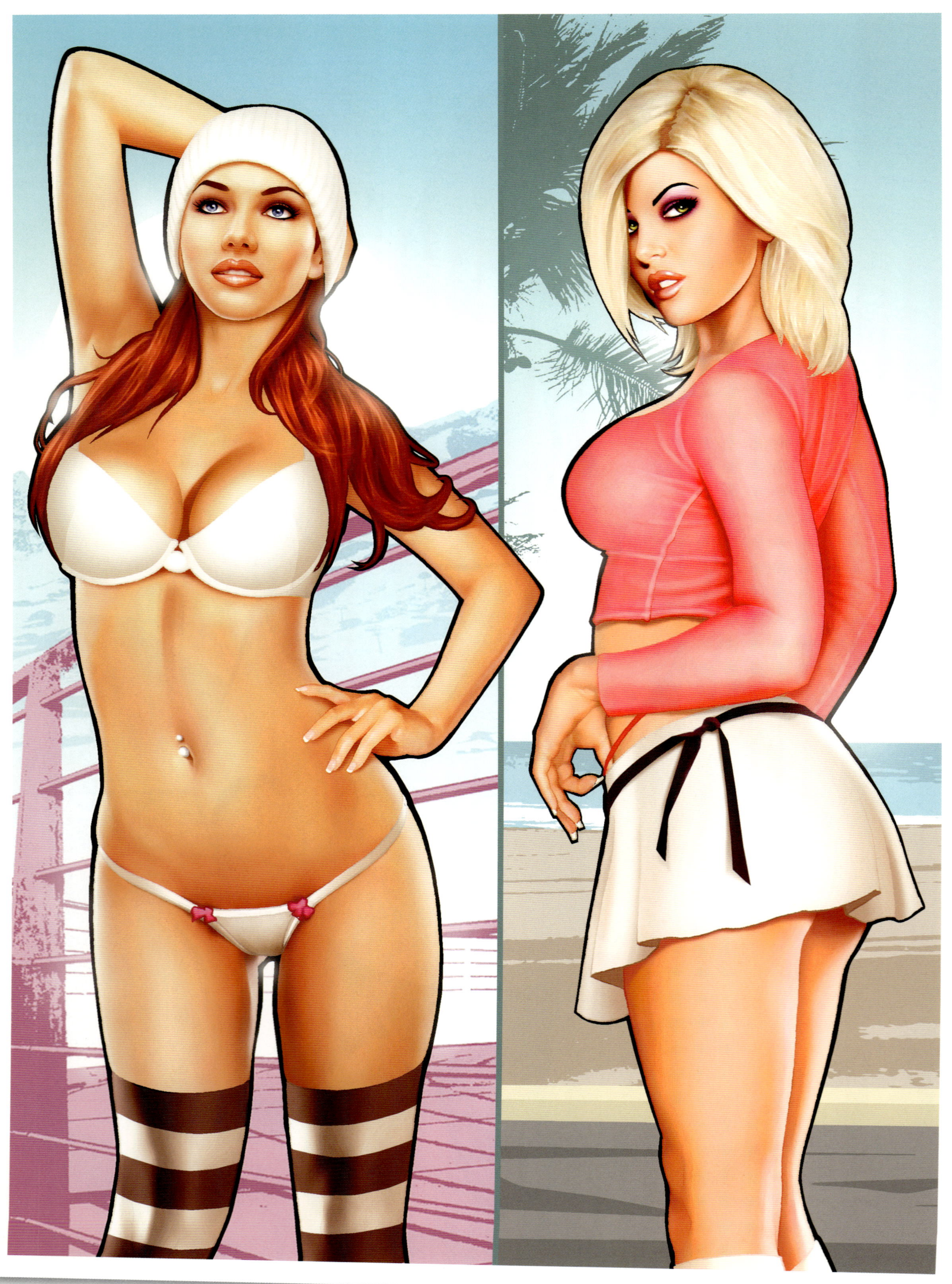

Kristy and JoJo shared a LOT more than a 3-week beach rental that summer! Yeee-OUCH!

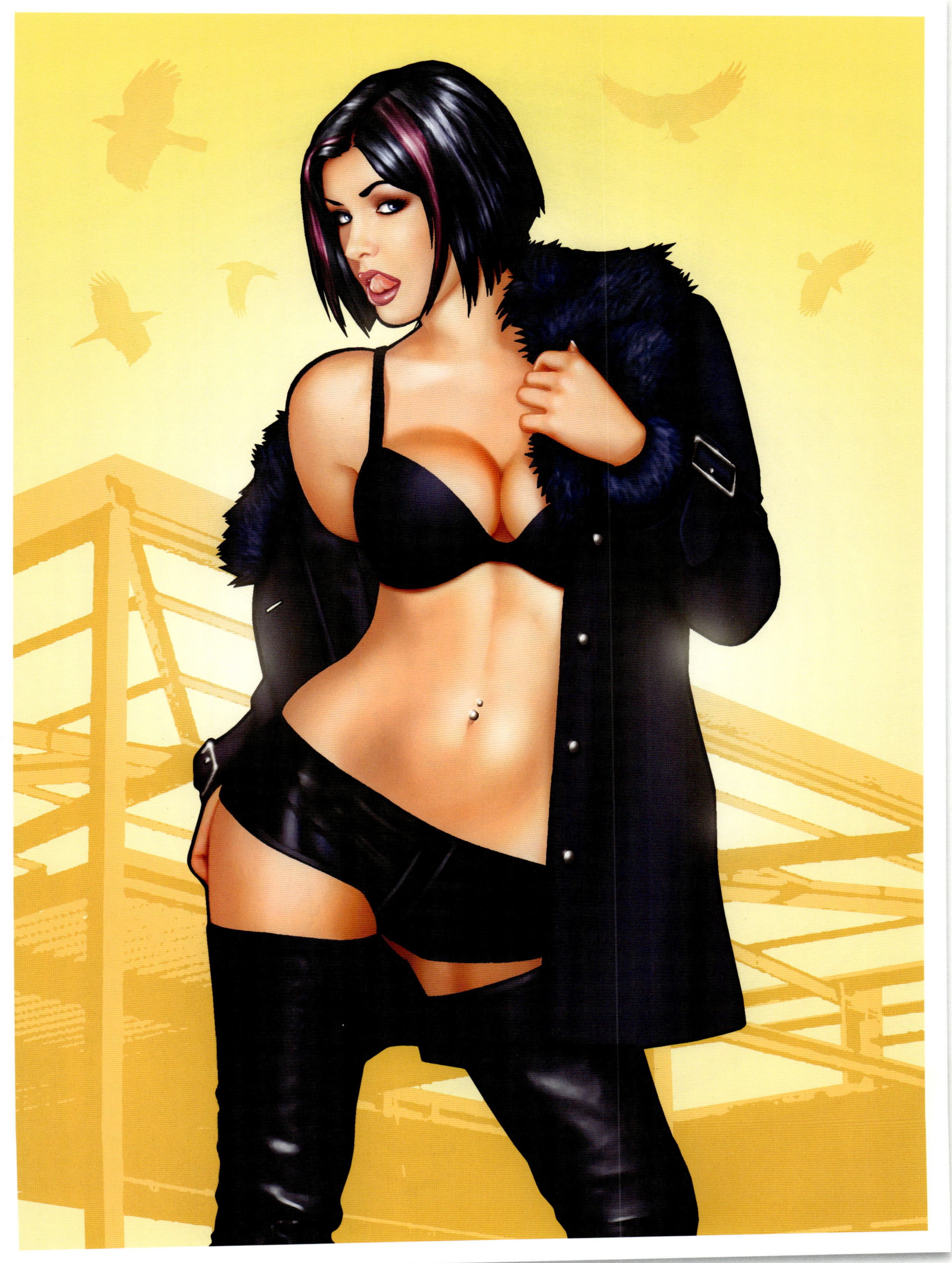

Ronnie was SUCH a bad girl - she left marks I'm STILL wearing!

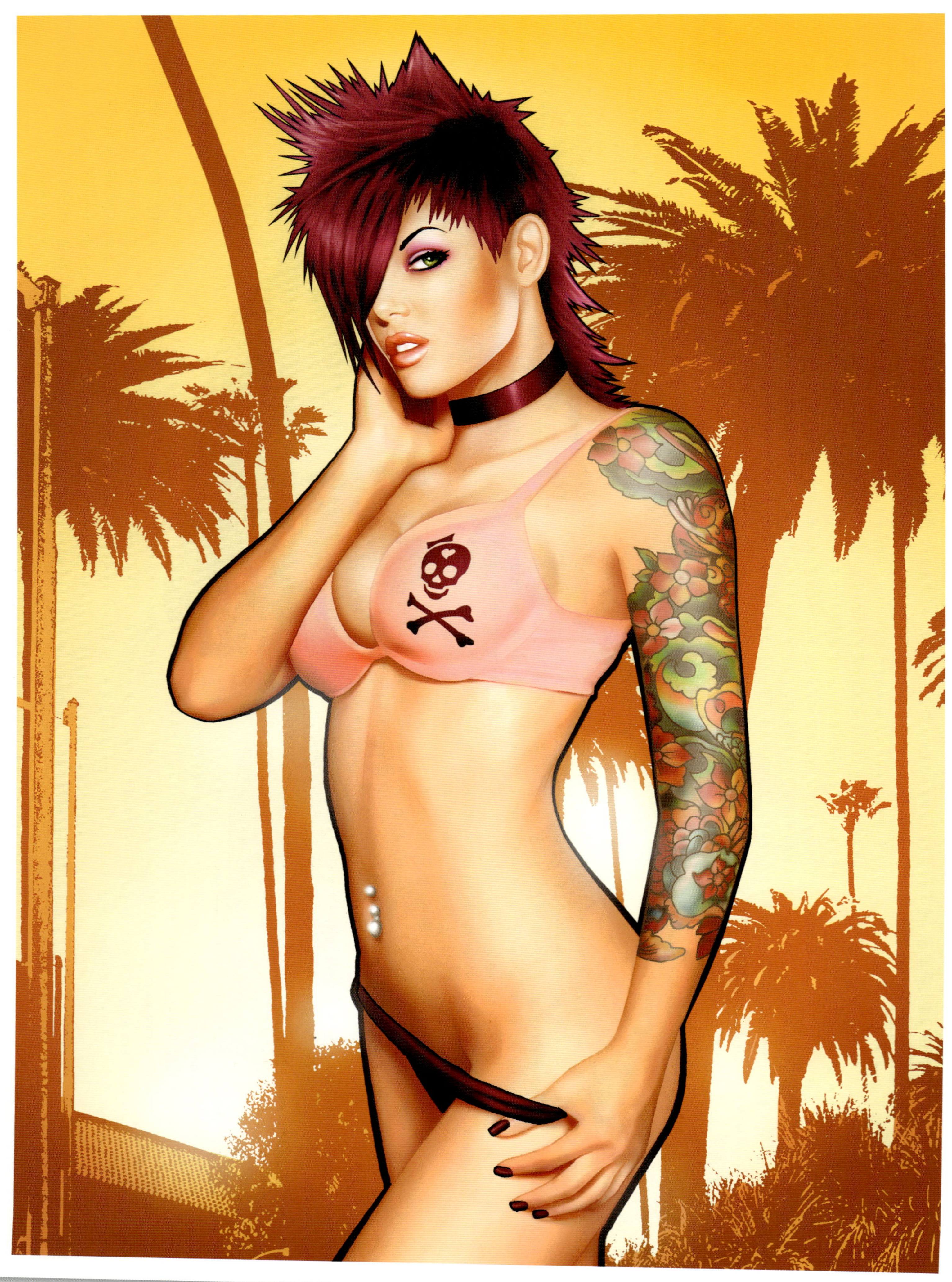

Dennie - a preacher's daughter with a seriously nasty attitude - trying to make up for so much lost time!

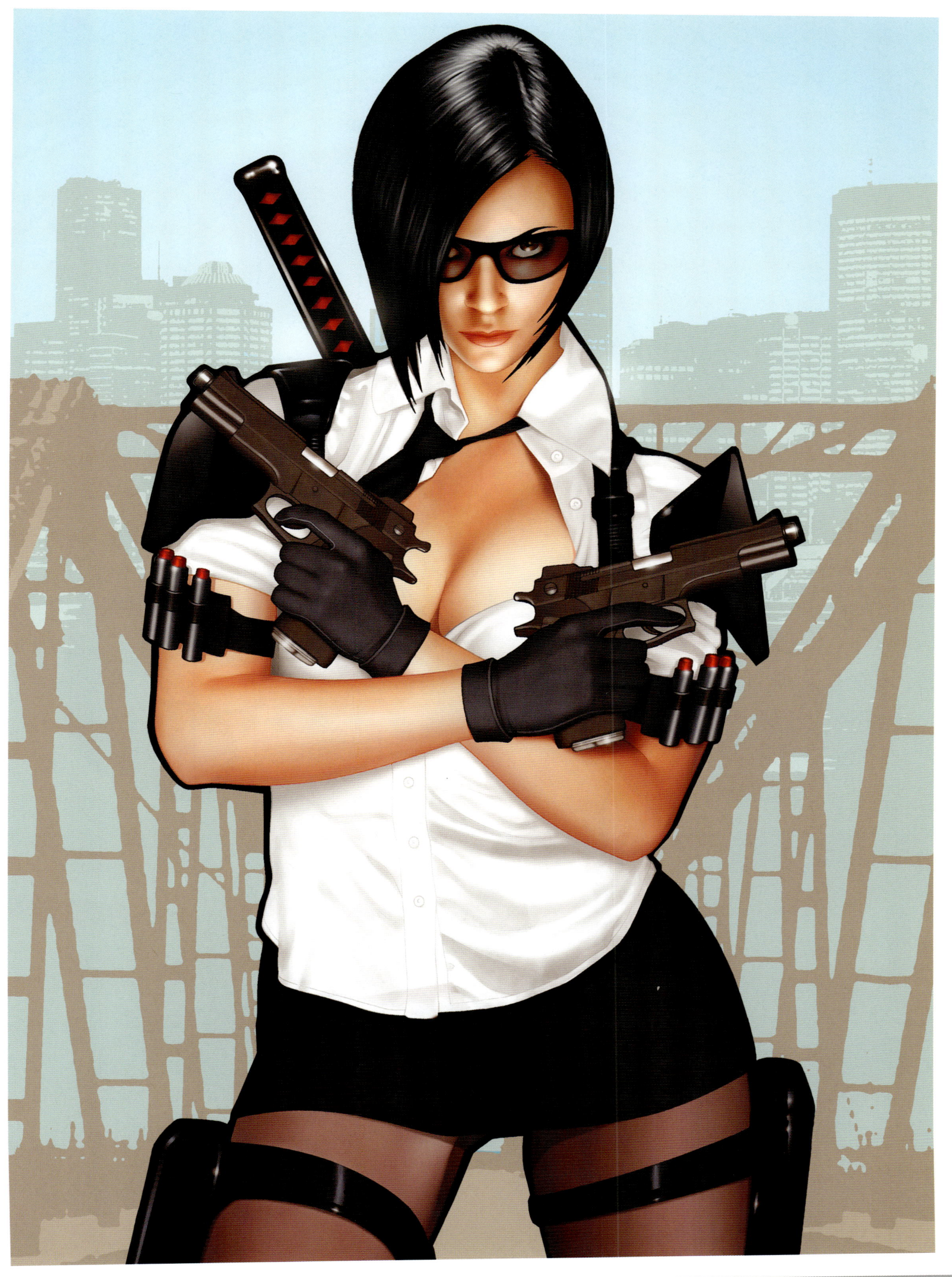

Model turned stuntwoman turned actress - turned ME everyway but loose! Hooray for Hollywood!

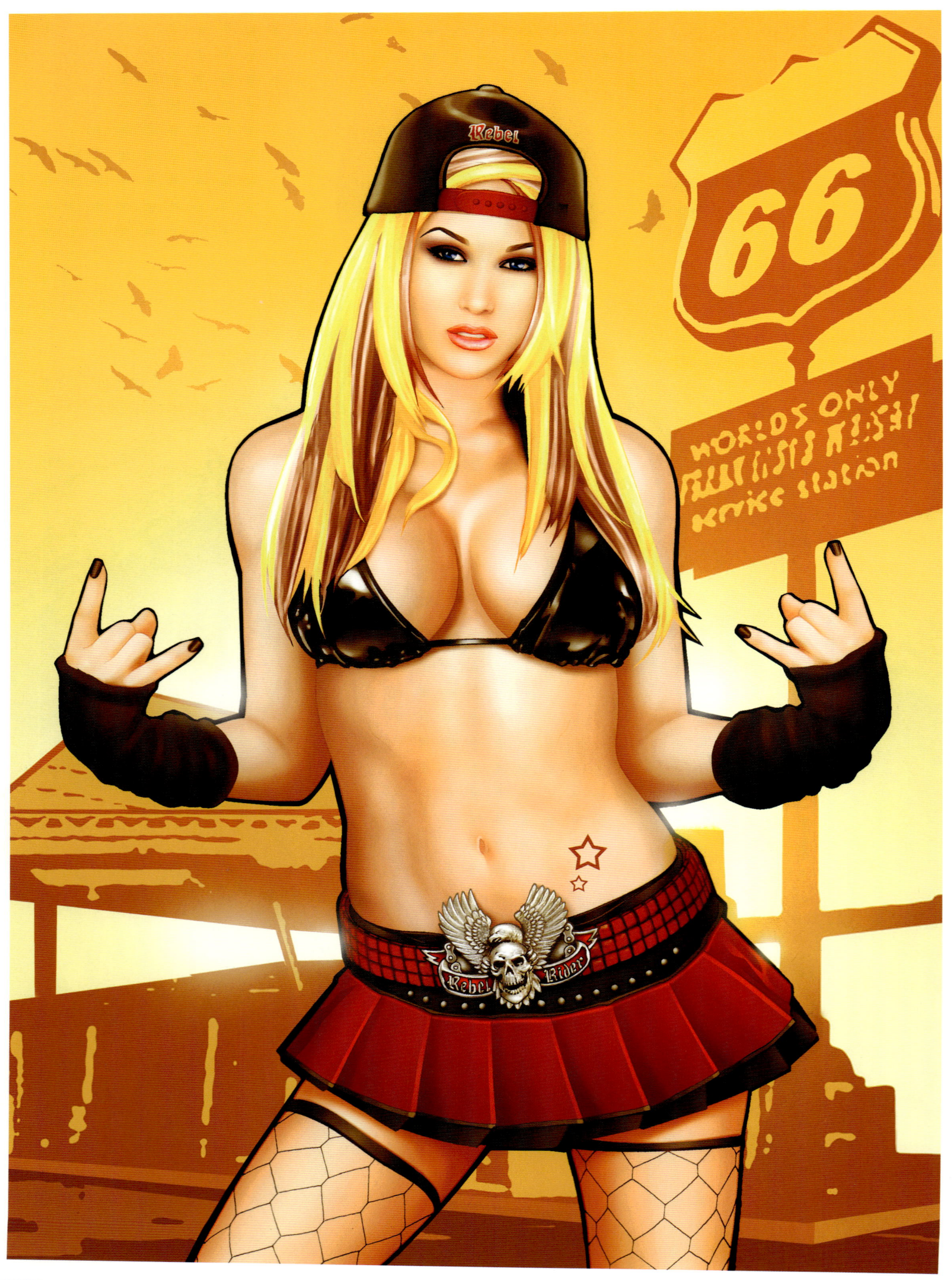

Got my kicks (and the best engine-overhaul of my life!) on Route 66. Thanks Becky!

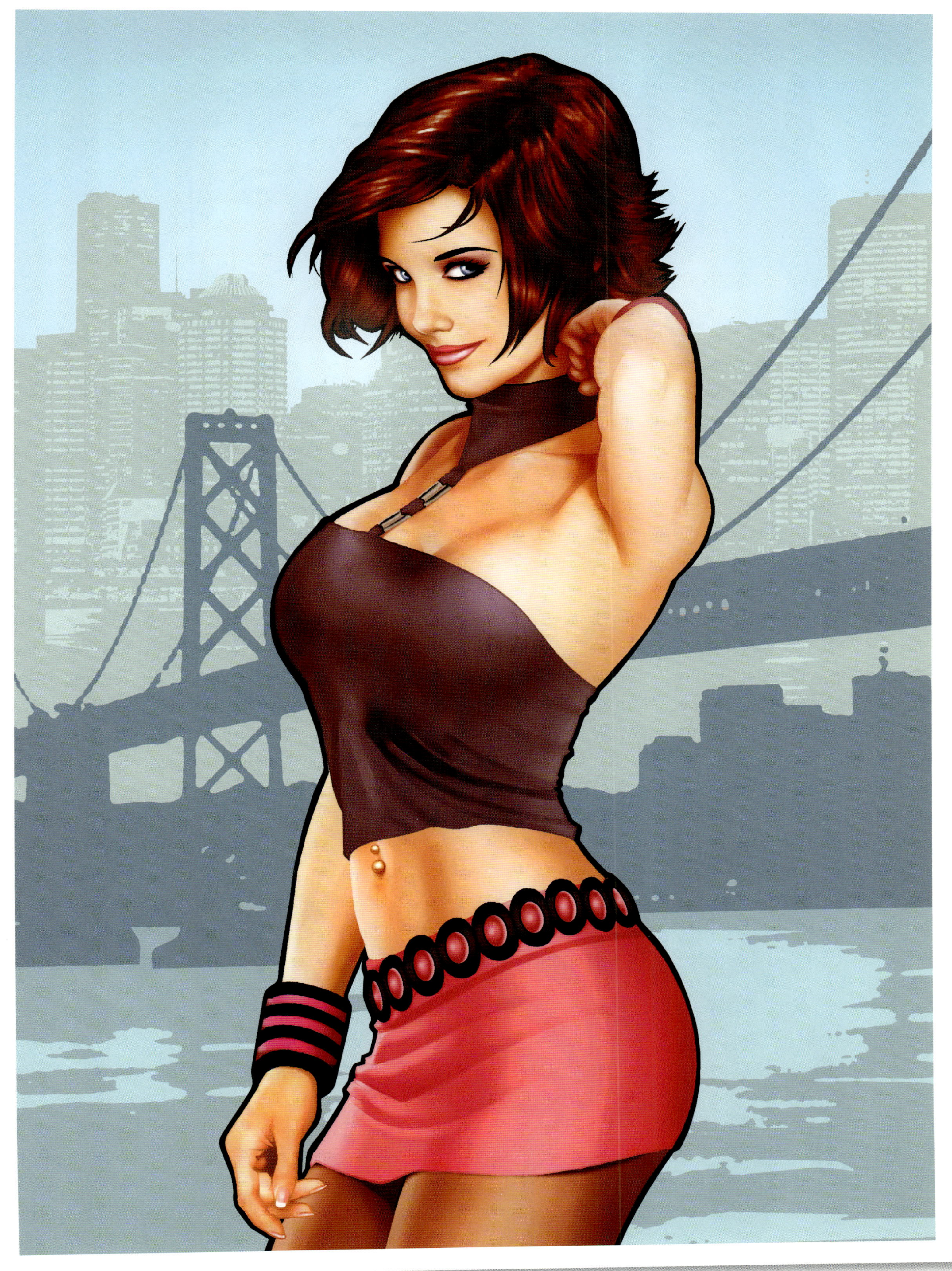

Chelsey was the ultimate "Girl-Next-Door" - if you happen to live next to Heaven!

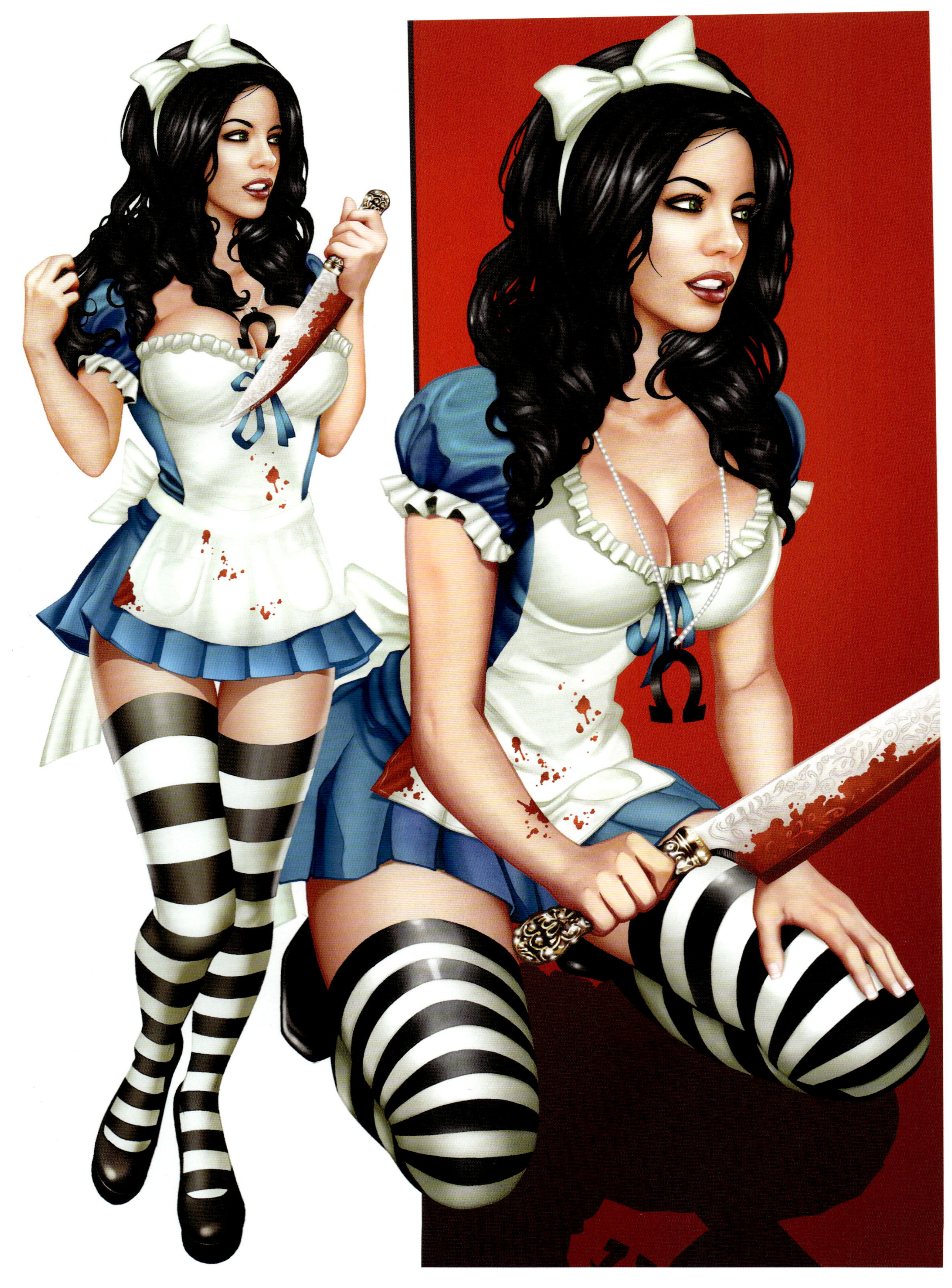

There's CosPlay, sexy CosPlay, and borderline dangerous sexy CosPlay. Darlene knew just how far to take it. Love that Darlene!

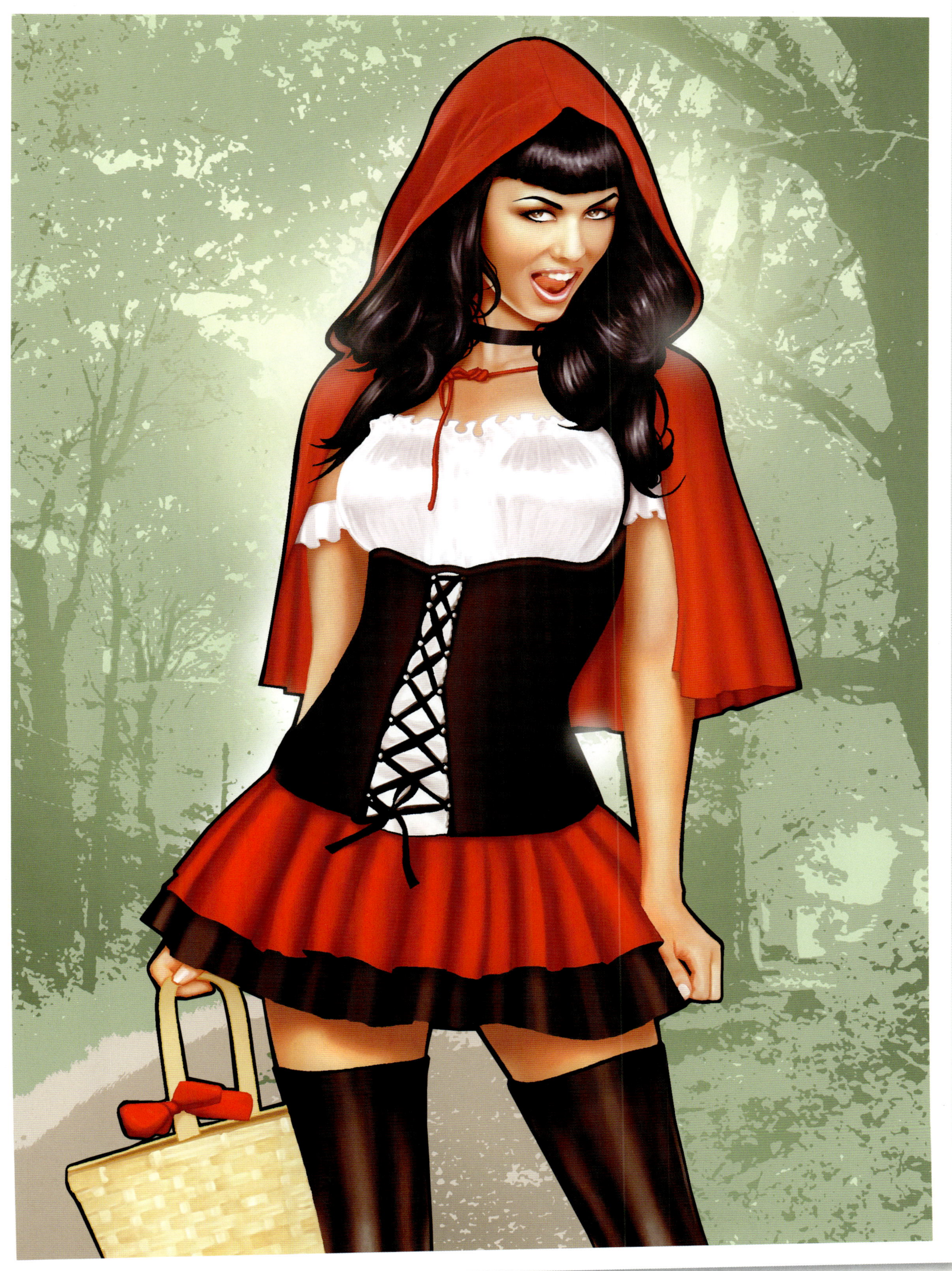

Oh, what Little Red had in her basket! This big bad wolf will never tell...

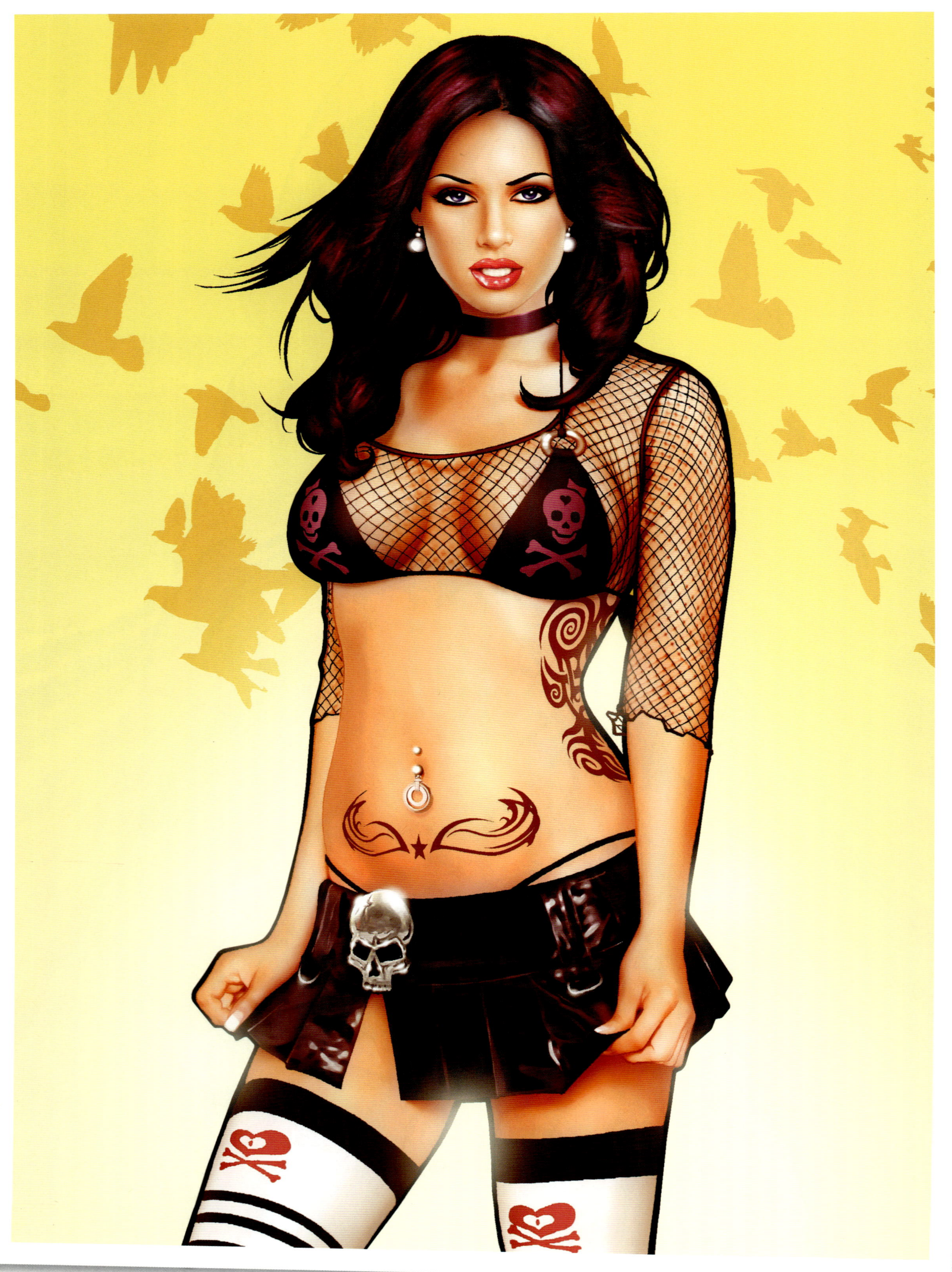

You meet the most interesting folk at 5:45AM leaving a biker bar! Sammi drank ALL the big boys under the table and looked THIS good doing it!

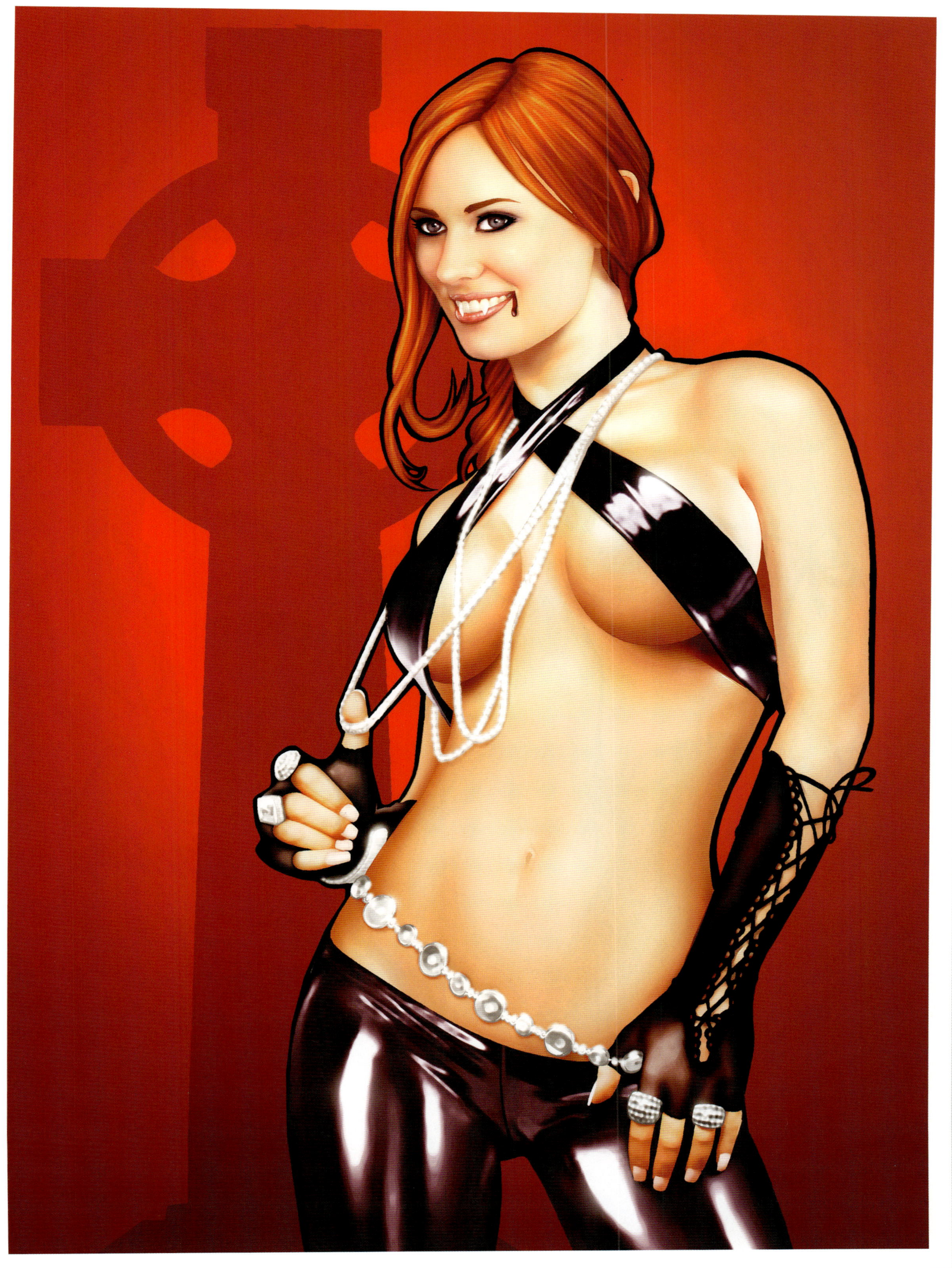

Met this one in a little diner in Louisiana. Loved the nightlife (but she wore SO much sunblock!)

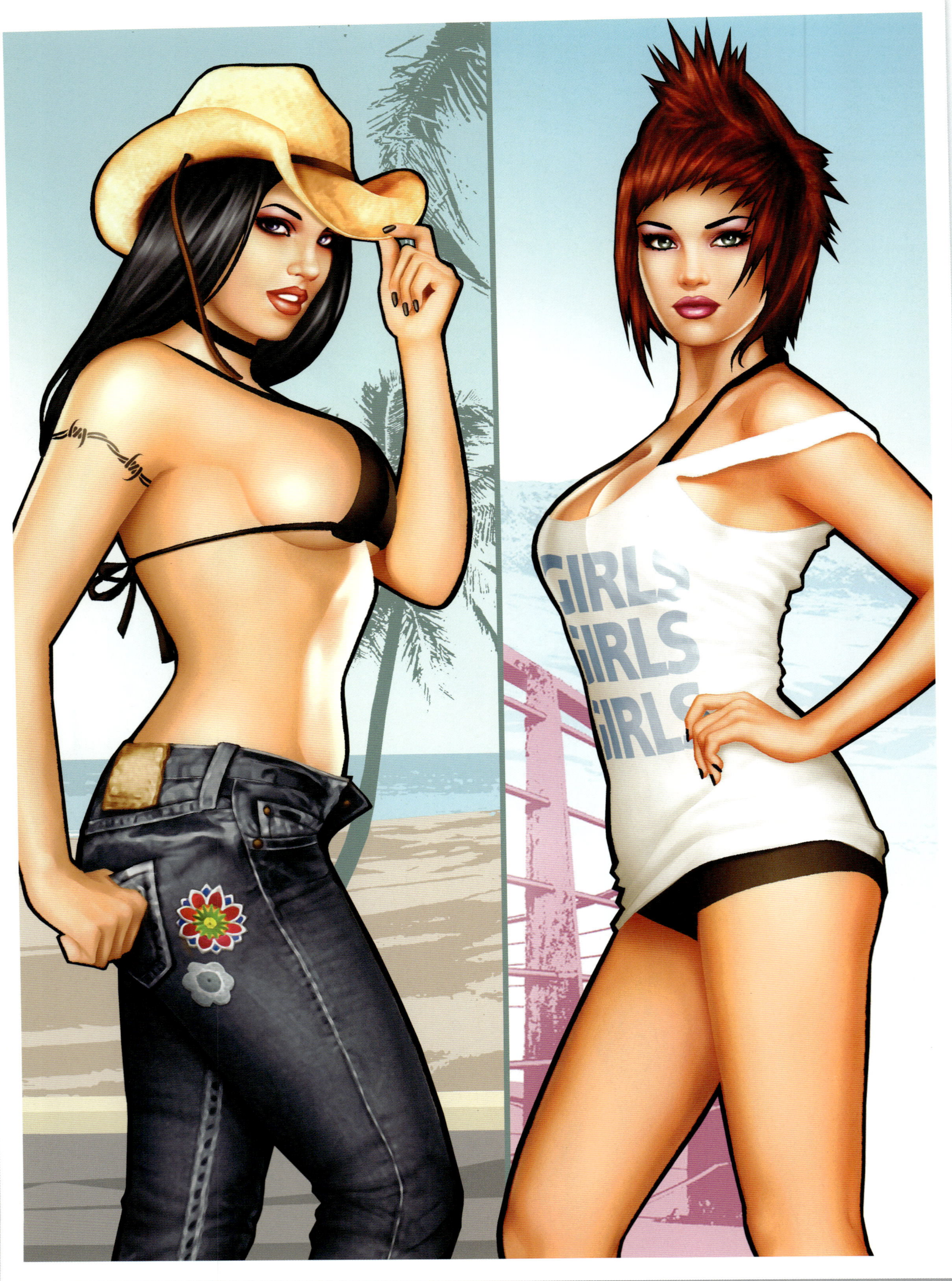

A couple of college students that taught me PLENTY!

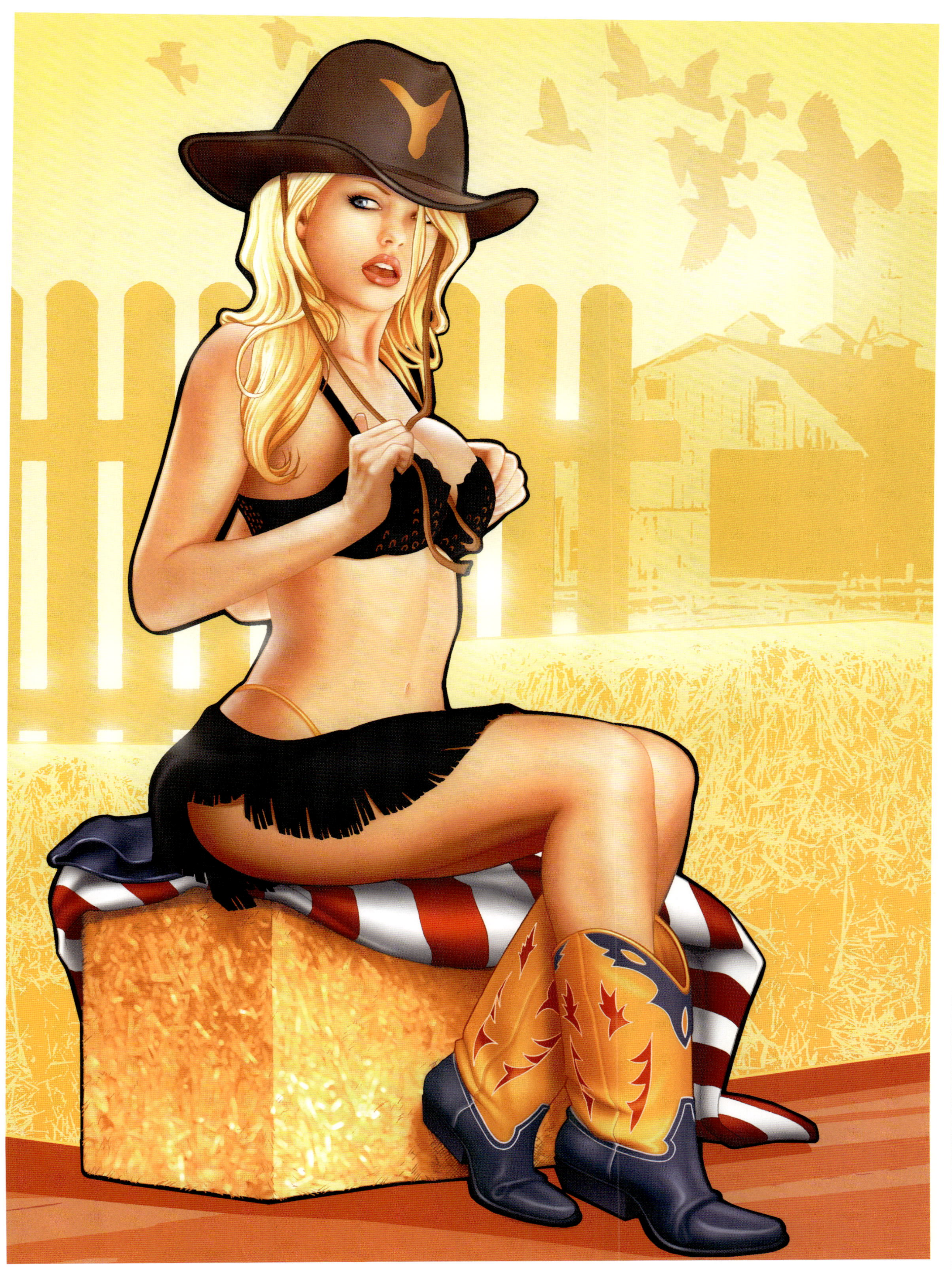

You don't mess with Texas - but you can sure have some fun there!

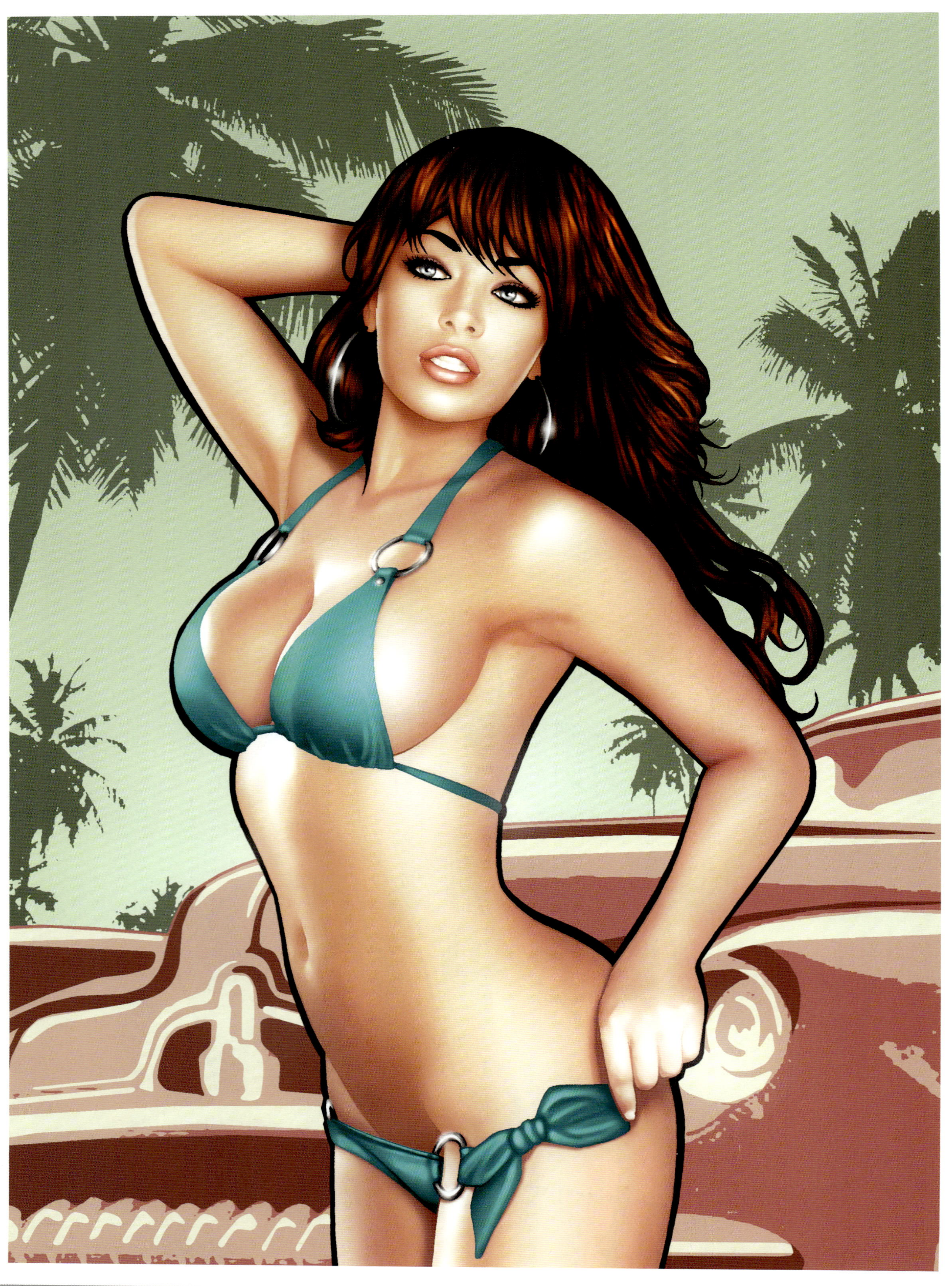

Maria was a lot like her classic car - she was gorgeous, powerful, and could go from zero to 60 in 12 seconds!

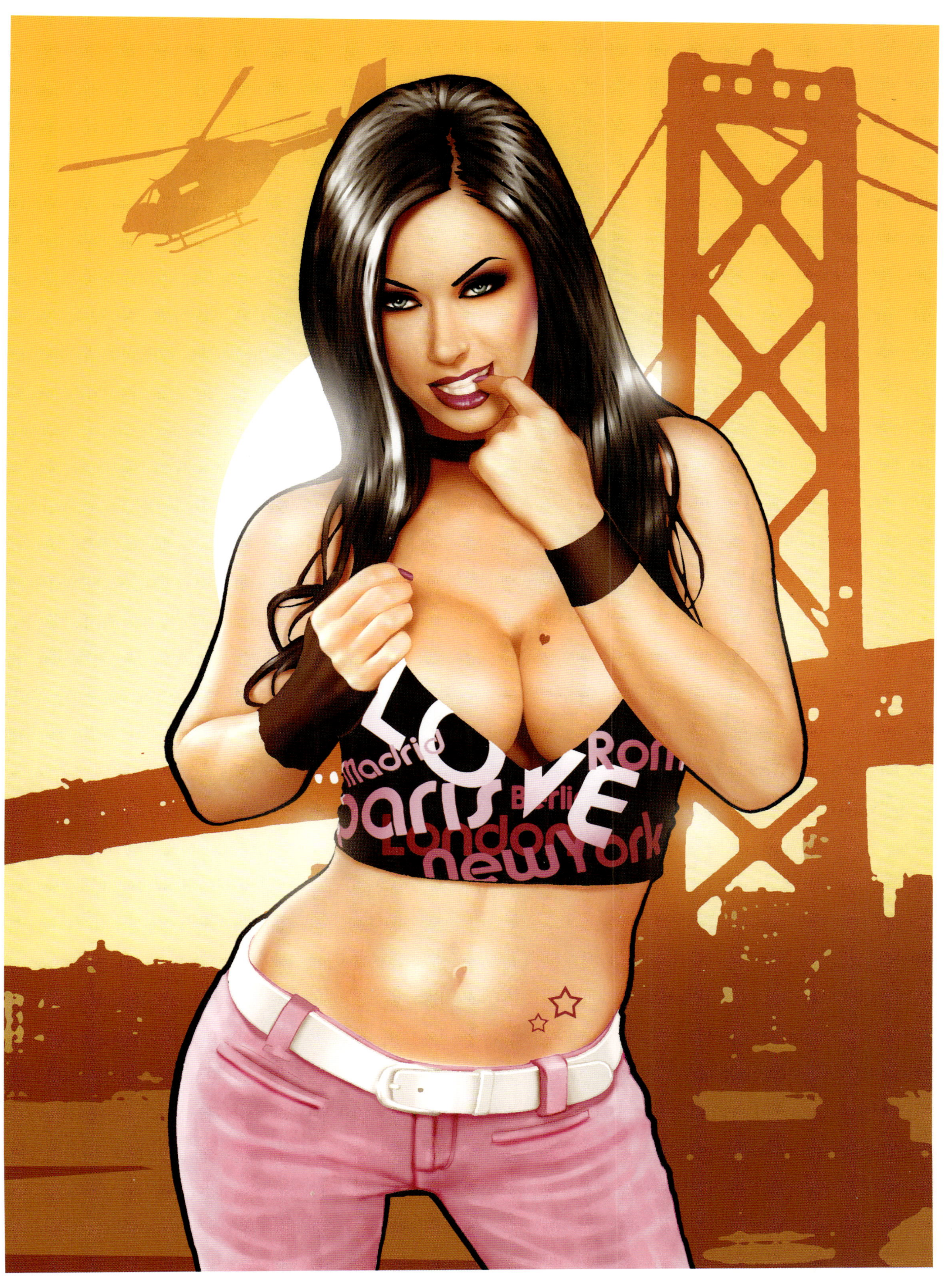

Penny liked to travel the world - collecting memories and breaking hearts. She's got frequent flyer miles in the millions!

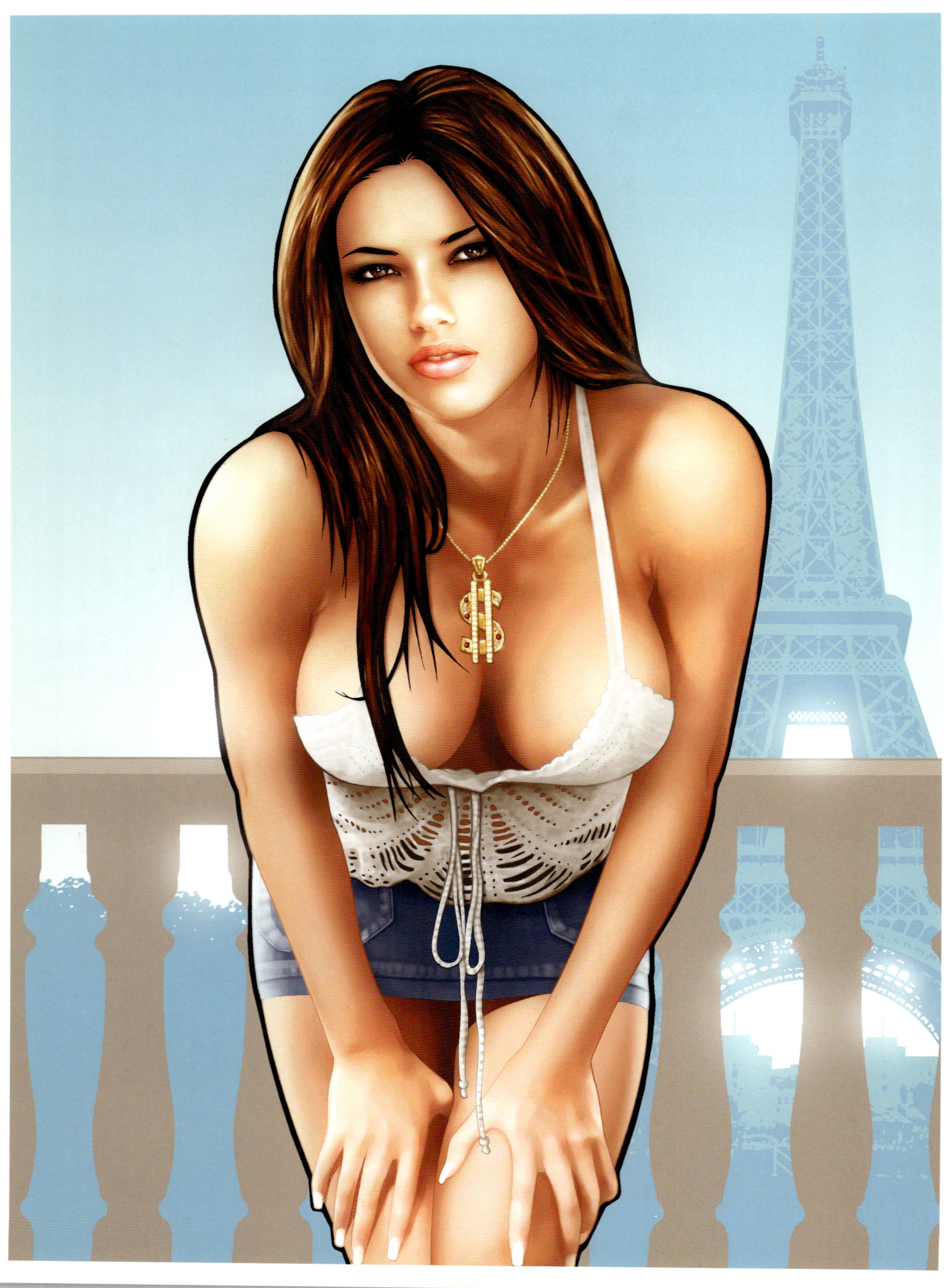

With an ass like Dominique's - no wonder that tower is standing straight up!

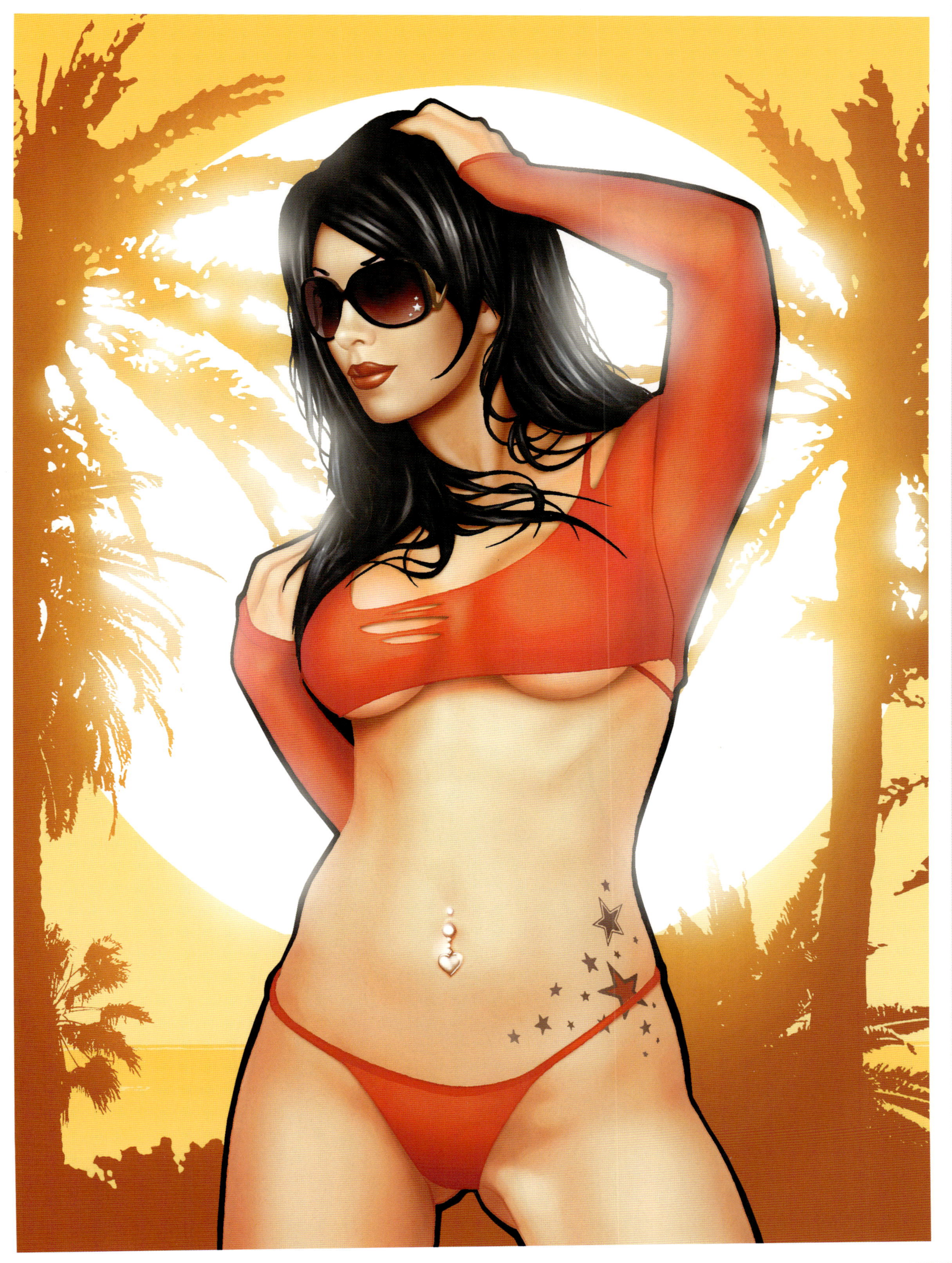

Kandi - she spent her time in Beverly Hills with the stars as, yeah - "Arm Kandi!"

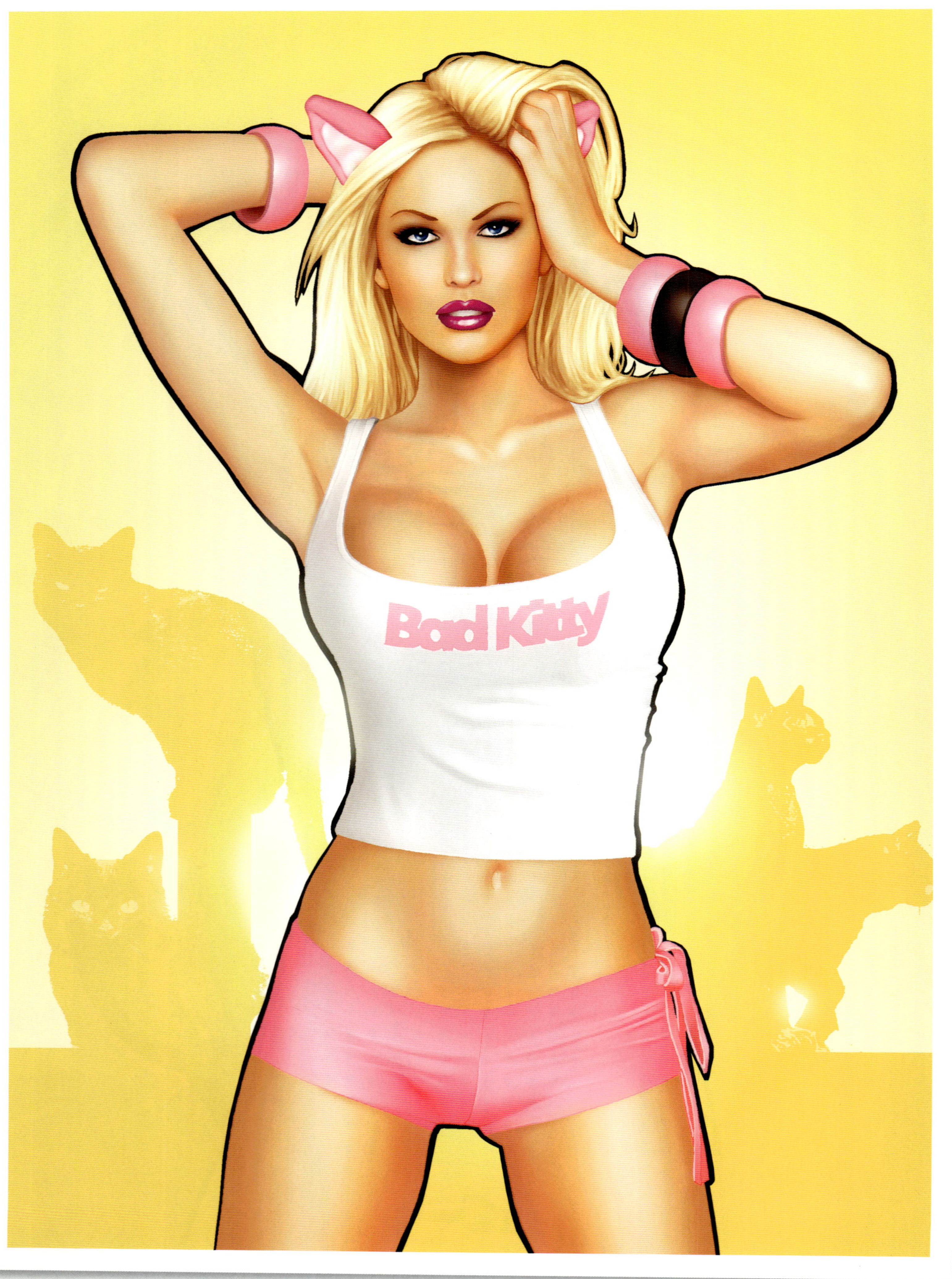

Land on all fours - get down on all fours - yep, she WAS a bad kitty! Oh, but to hear her purr - it was worth it!

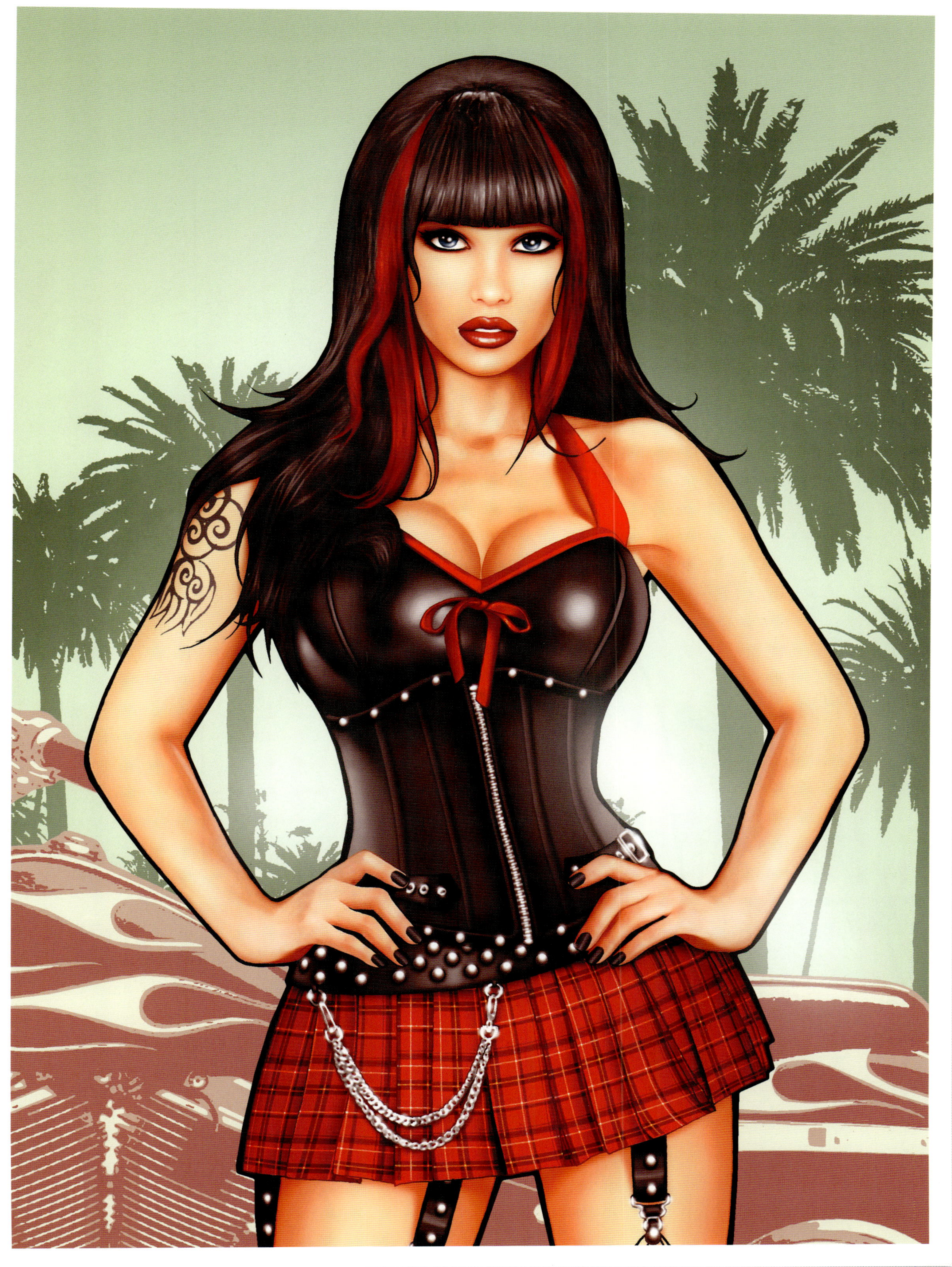

DeeDee was a public menace! Where ever she walked - at least ONE car would end up driving into a lamp post!

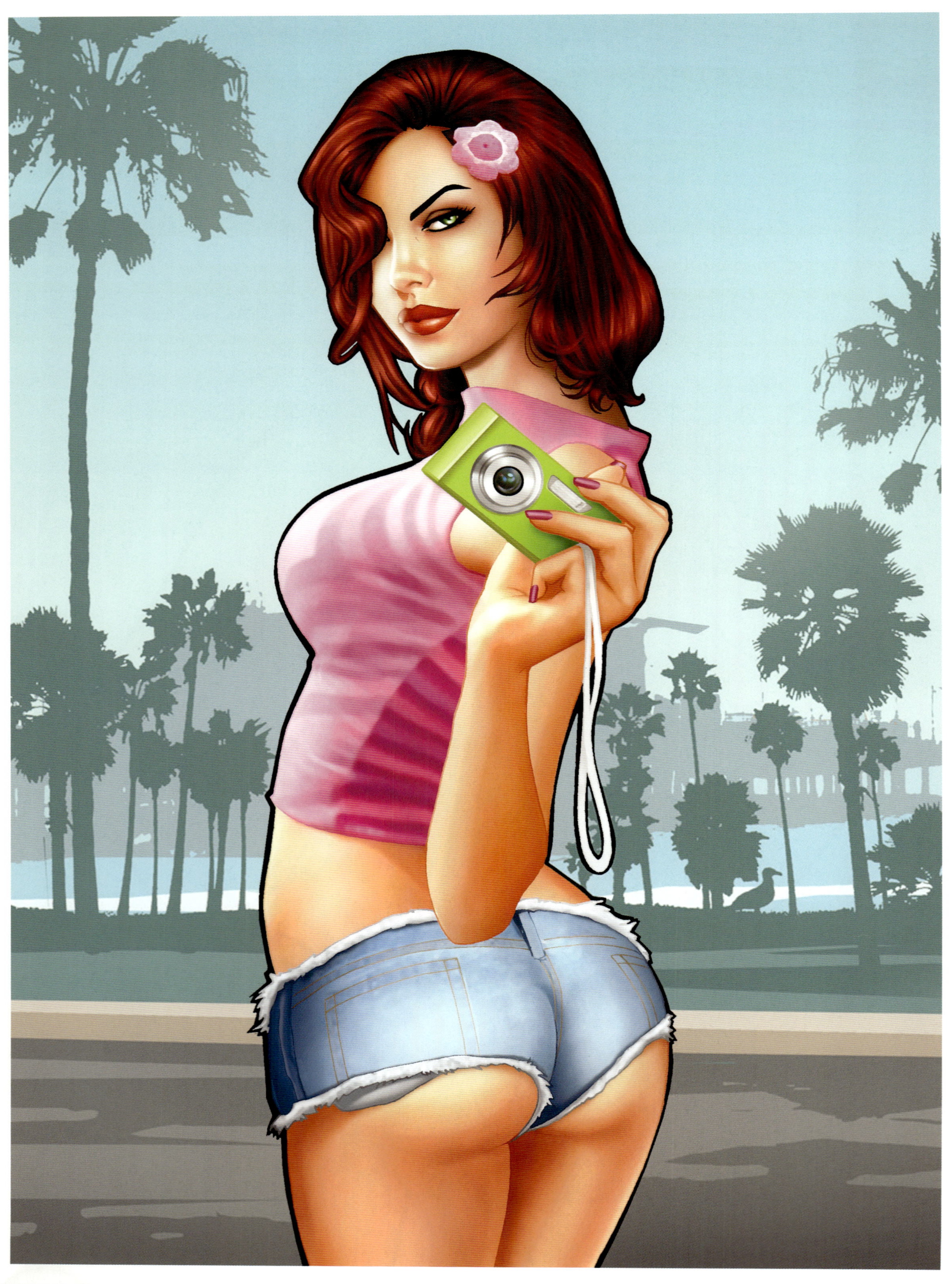

My first meeting with Kelly - "If you're gonna stare at my ass like that, you might as well get a good shot of it". And I did. Several times...

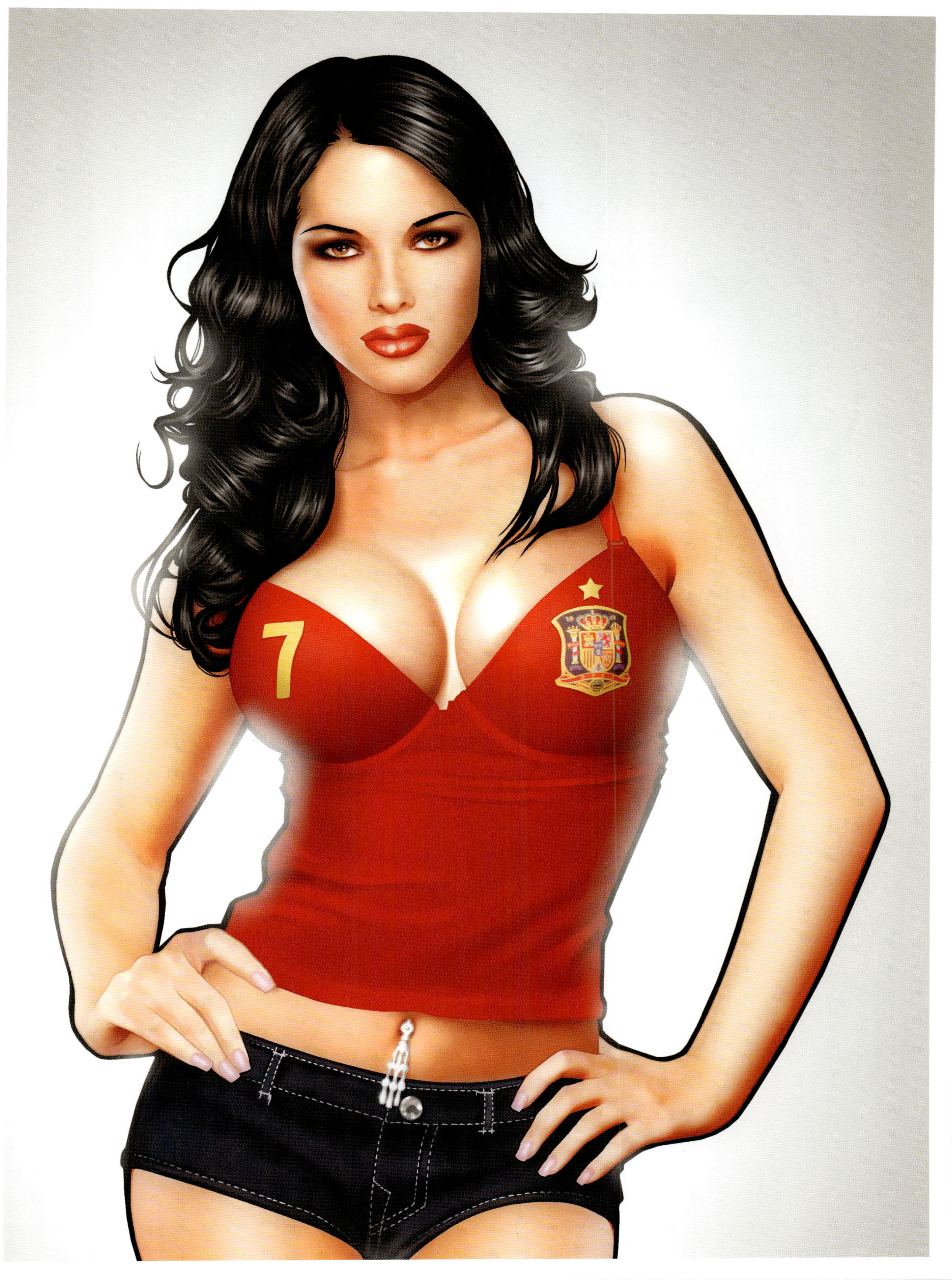

Fortunately, "7" has always been a lucky number for me.

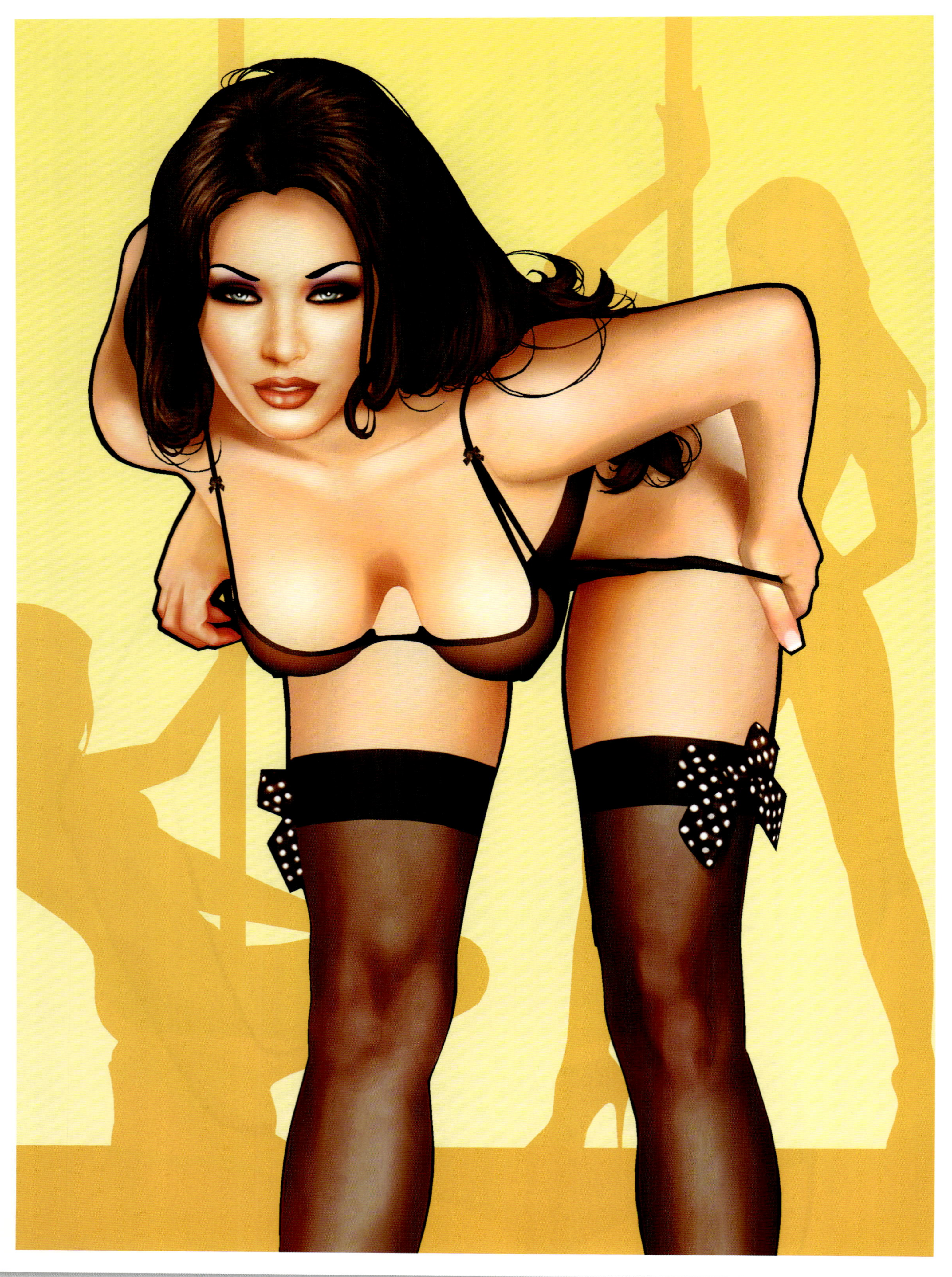

That night gets a little fuzzy. I DO remember paying the hotel room in single dollars.

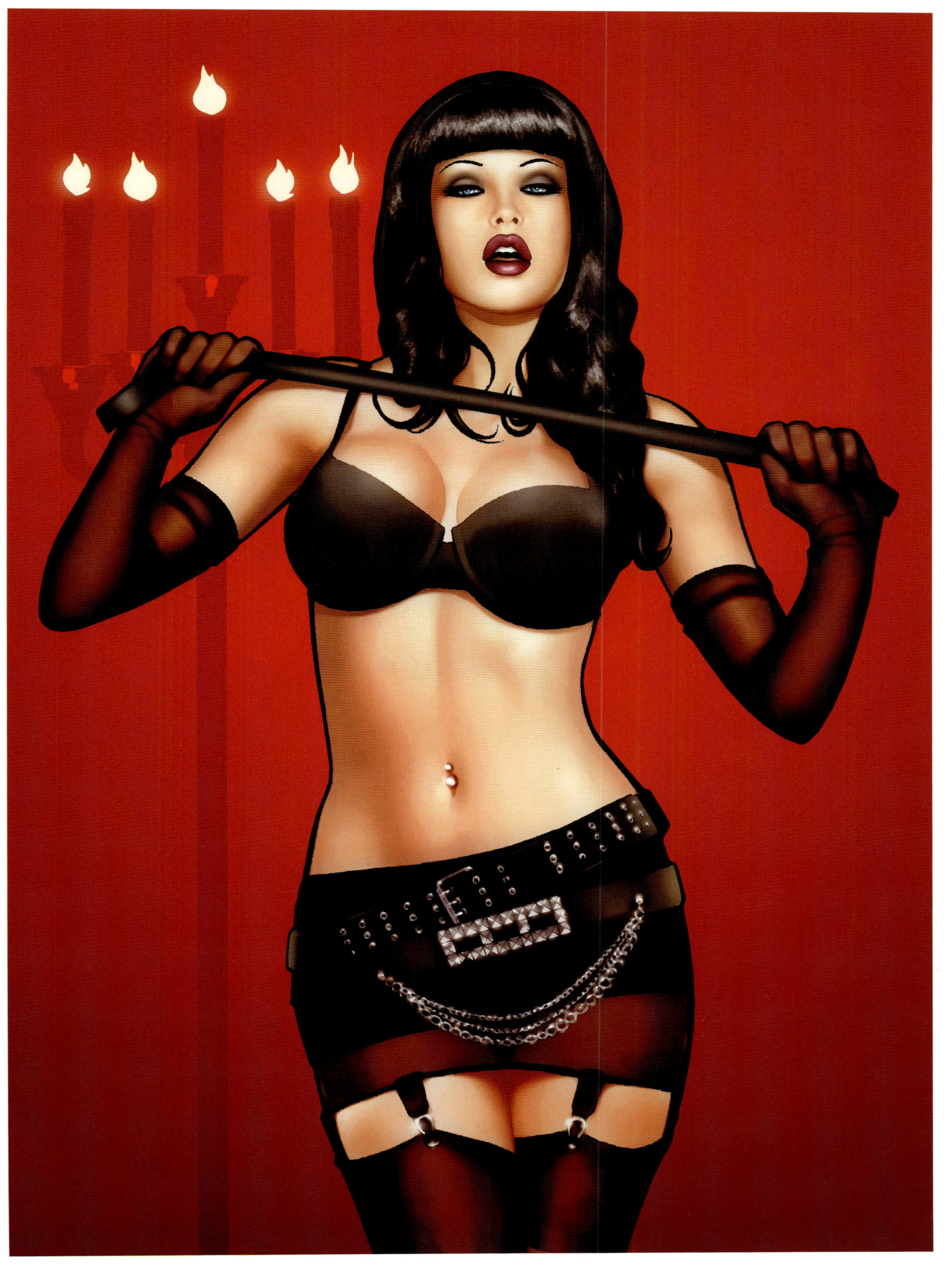

When you are as bad a boy as I have been, you have to be punished. Mistress Bianca knows me only too well!

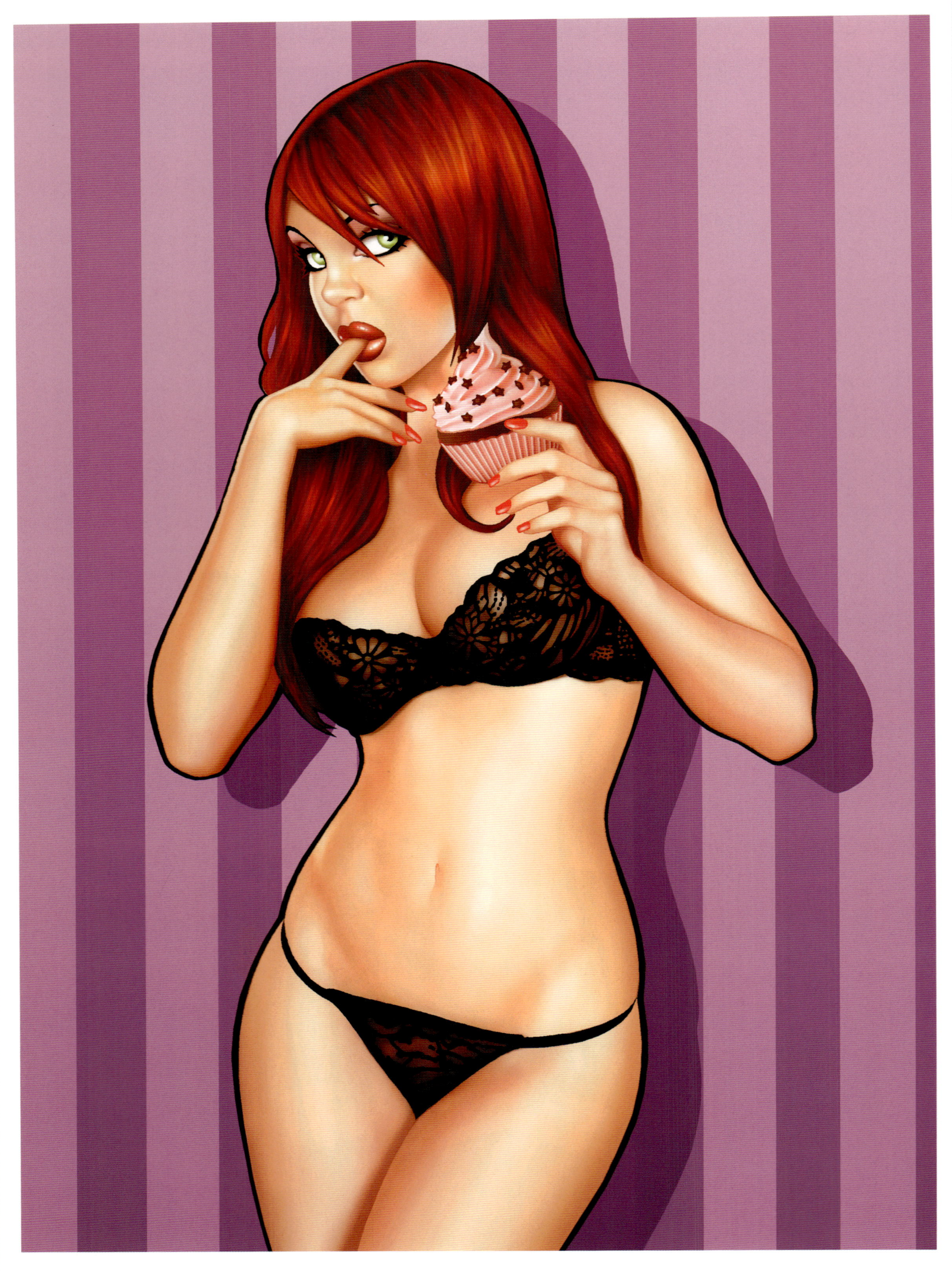

Yes, she ate that cupcake - but she insisted we work off those sinful calories together.

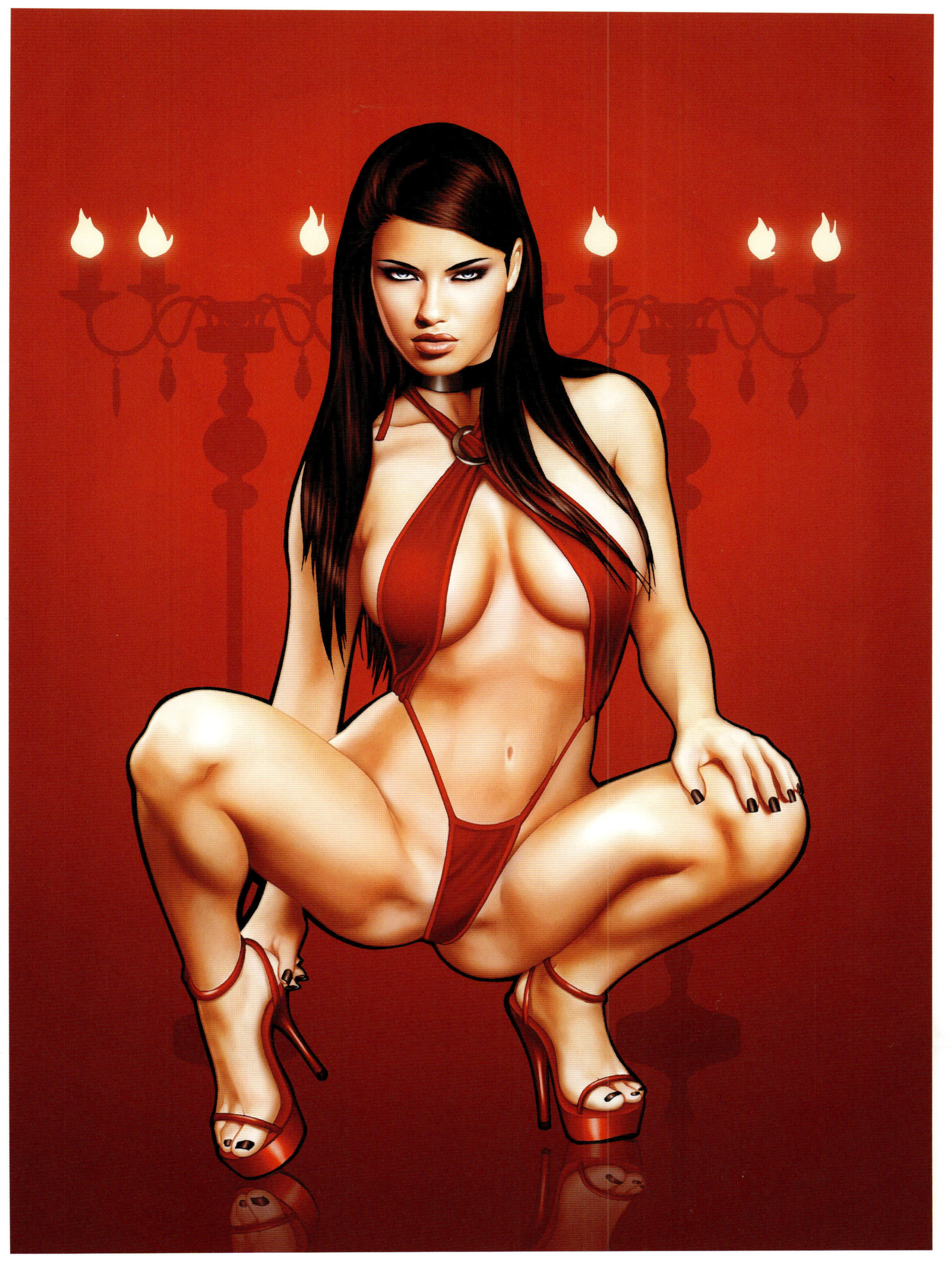

Don't remember much from that night - except waking up the next morning with holes in my neck and an empty wallet.

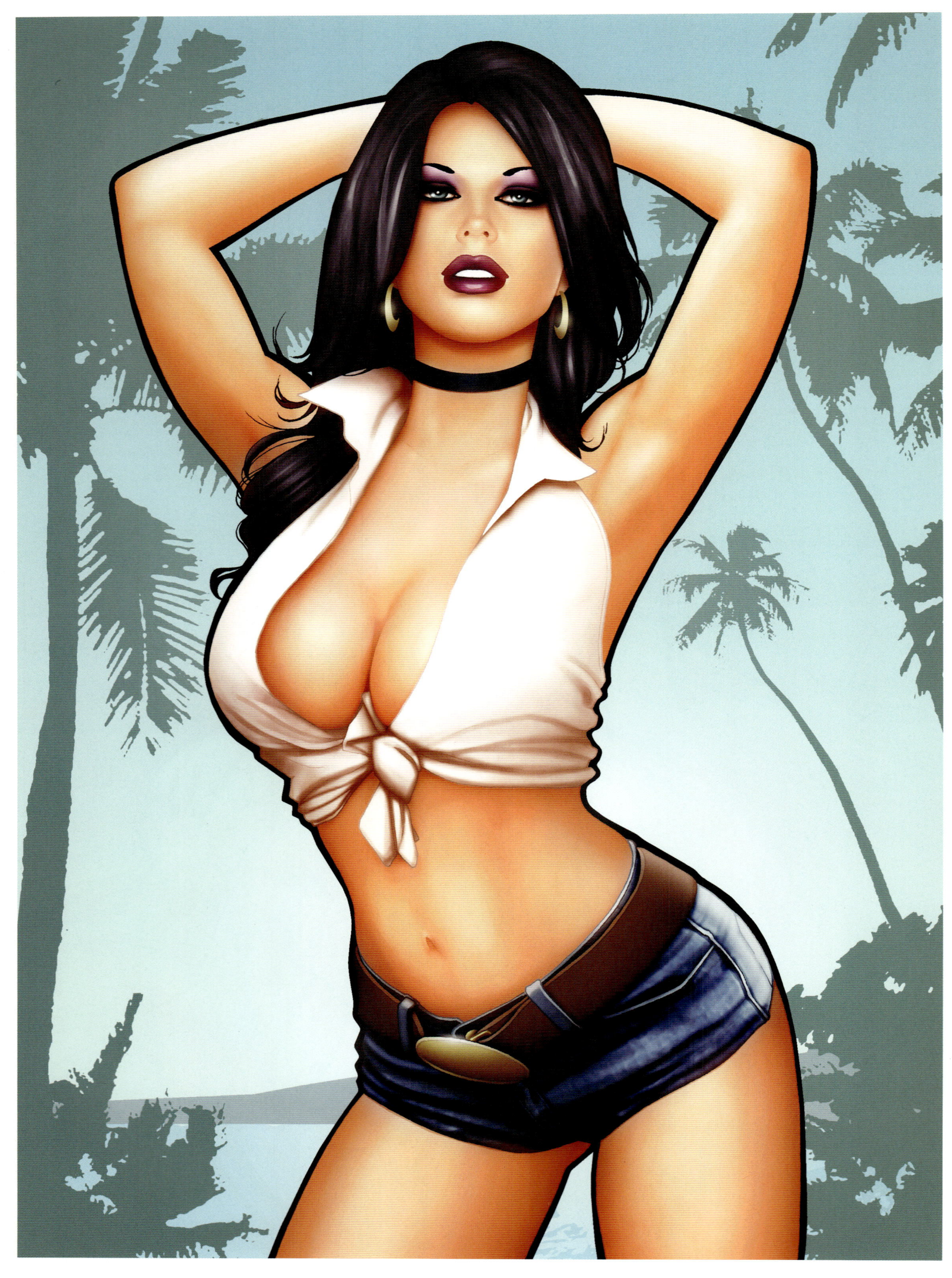

Florida was hot, sticky, and moist. Barbara-Anne was a lot like Florida! I'd visit Florida again ANYtime!

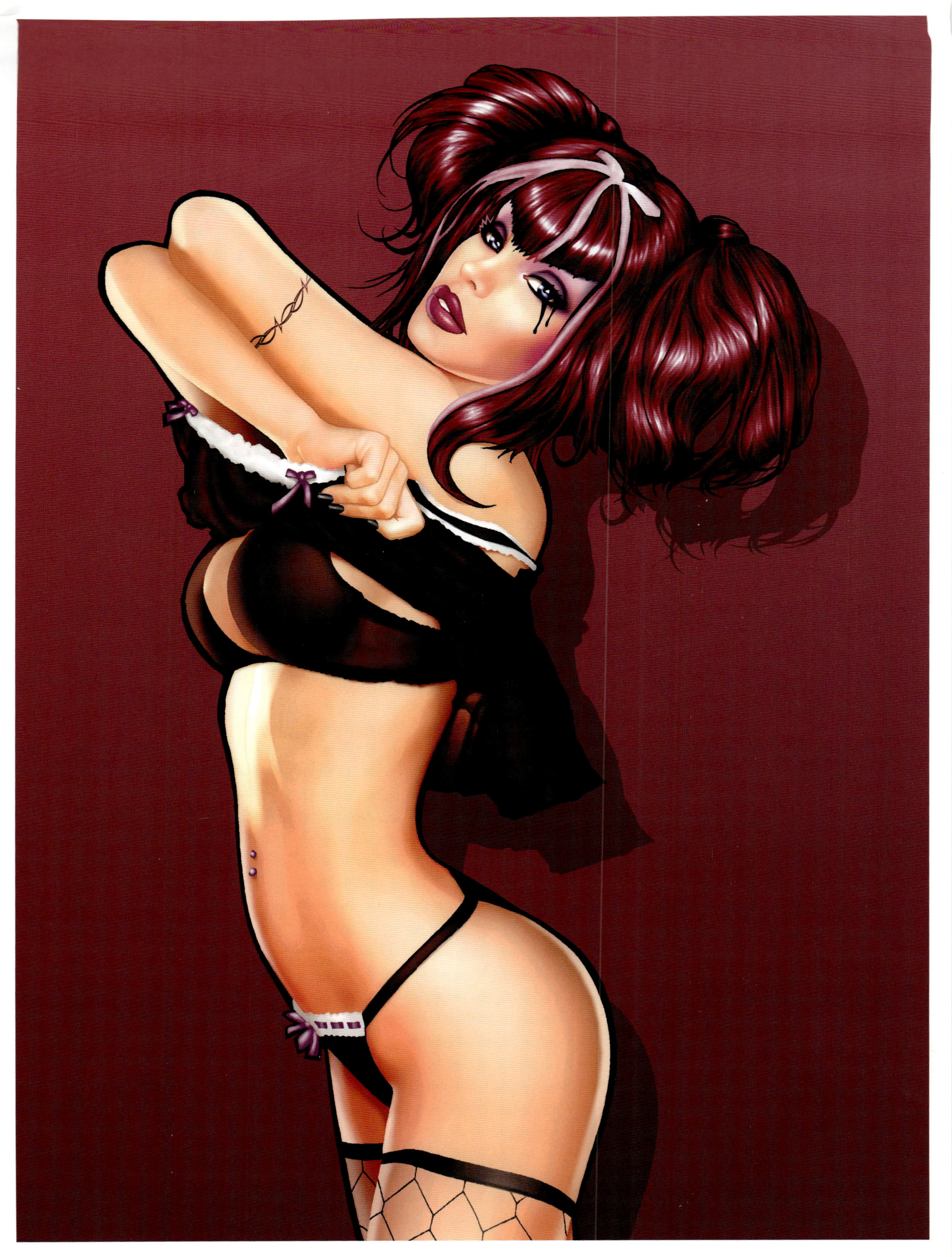

Kim could be a little moody - but what she lacked in emotional stabilty she more than made up in physical flexibility!

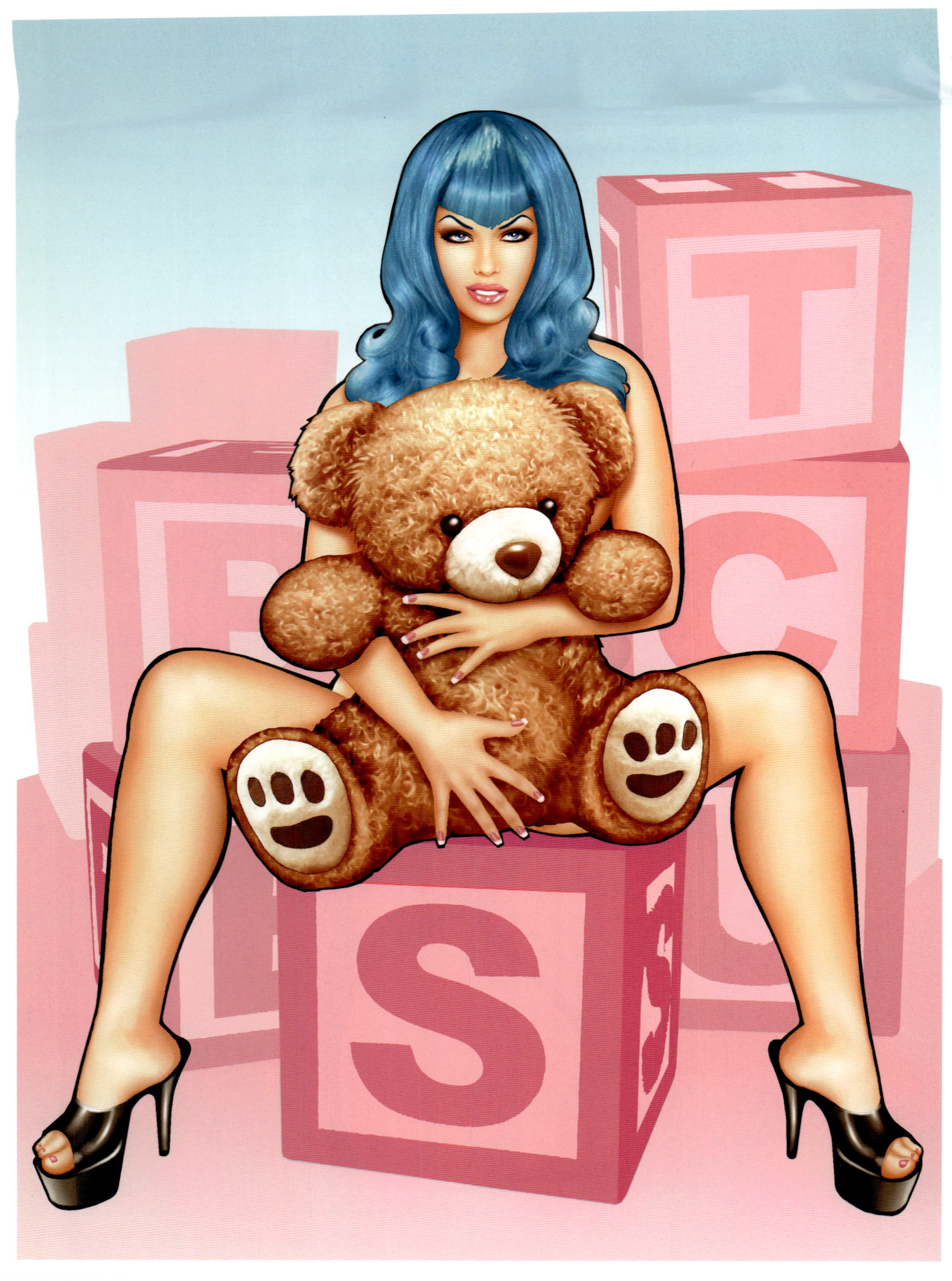

Penny liked to role-play. The bear liked to watch. Who was I to judge?

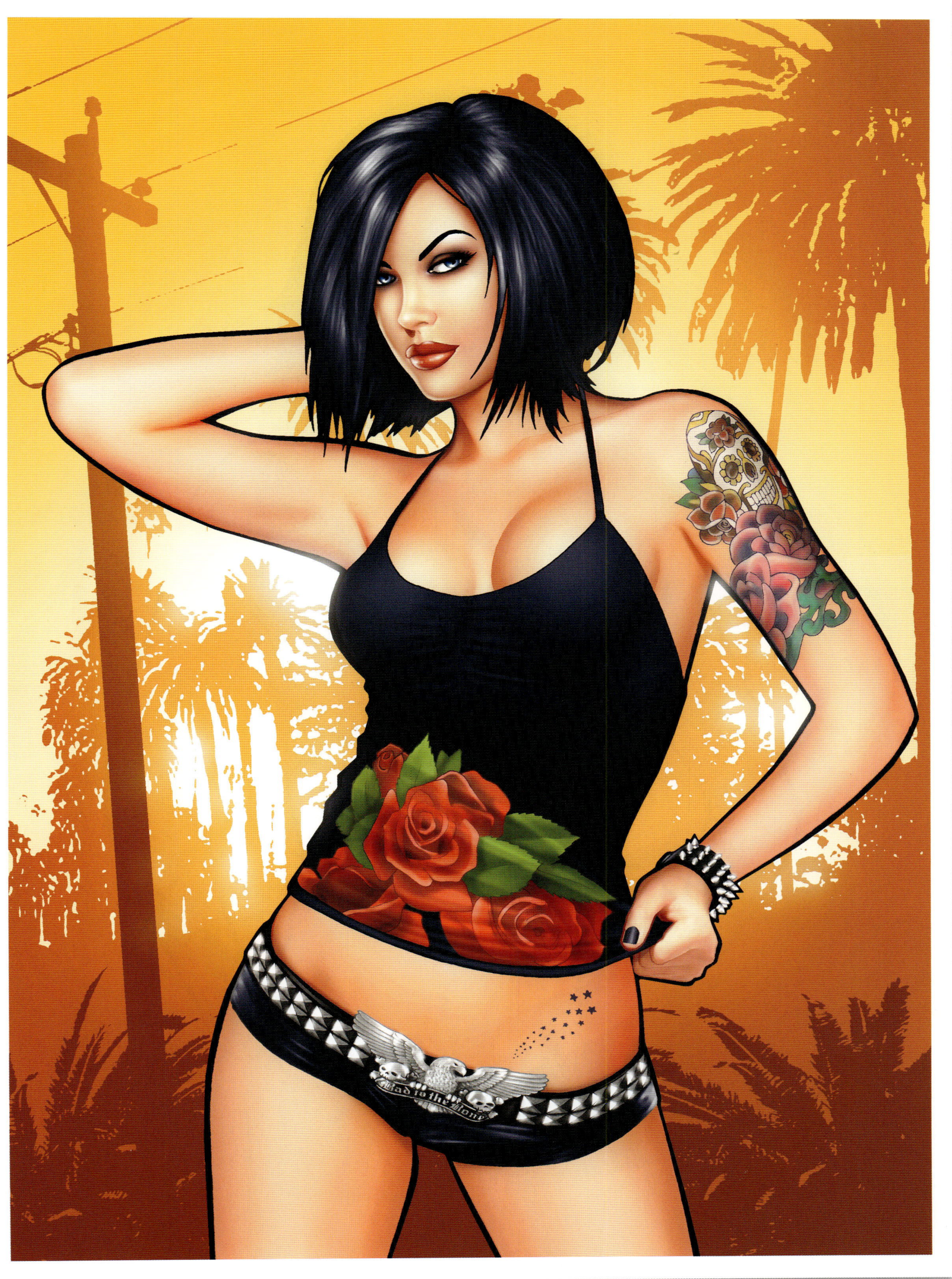

Monica was into ink. And artists. I came up with some interesting designs for her - but you can't see them in THIS pose!

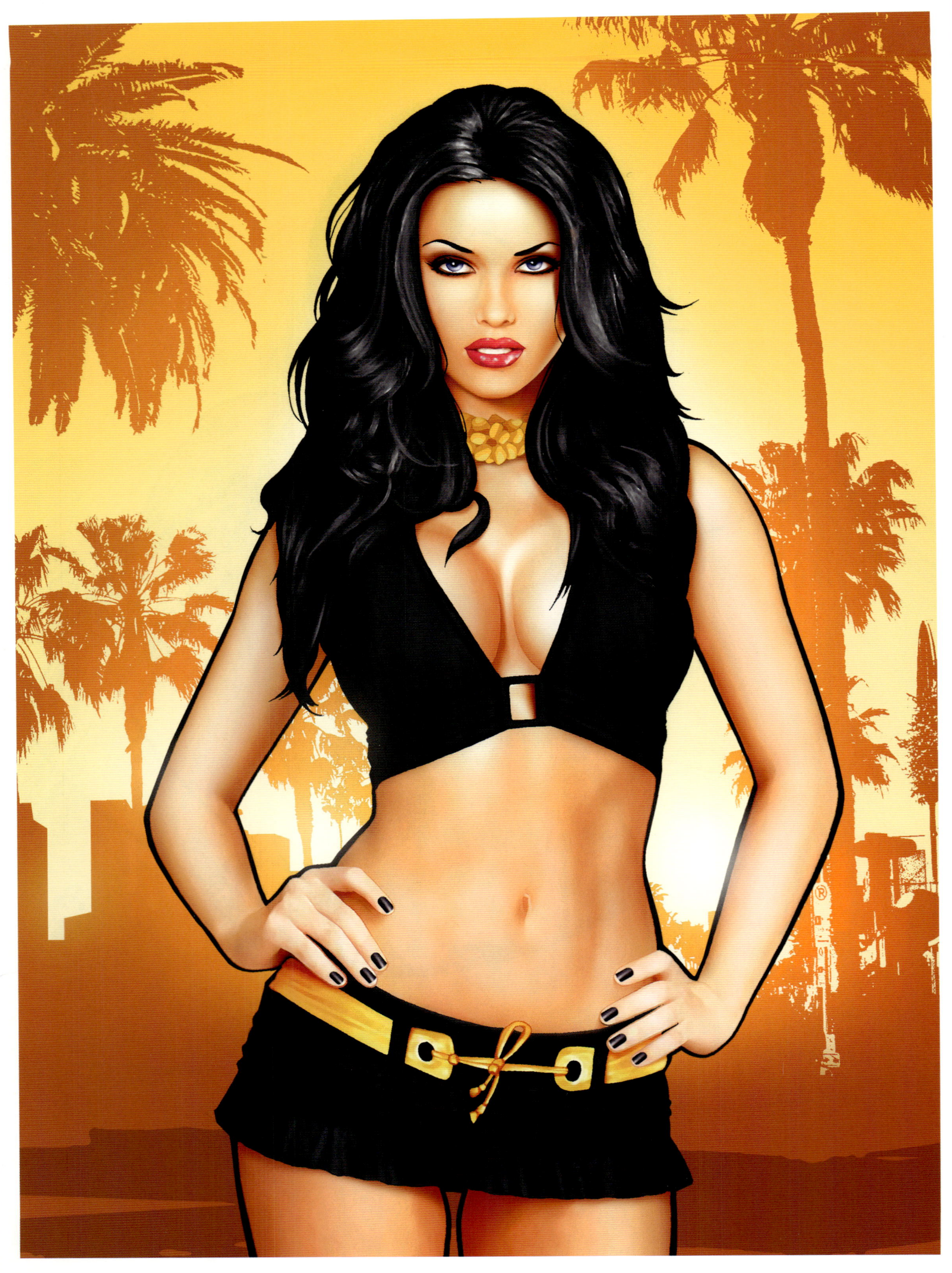

Sofia was a human blast furnace - melting everything in her path.

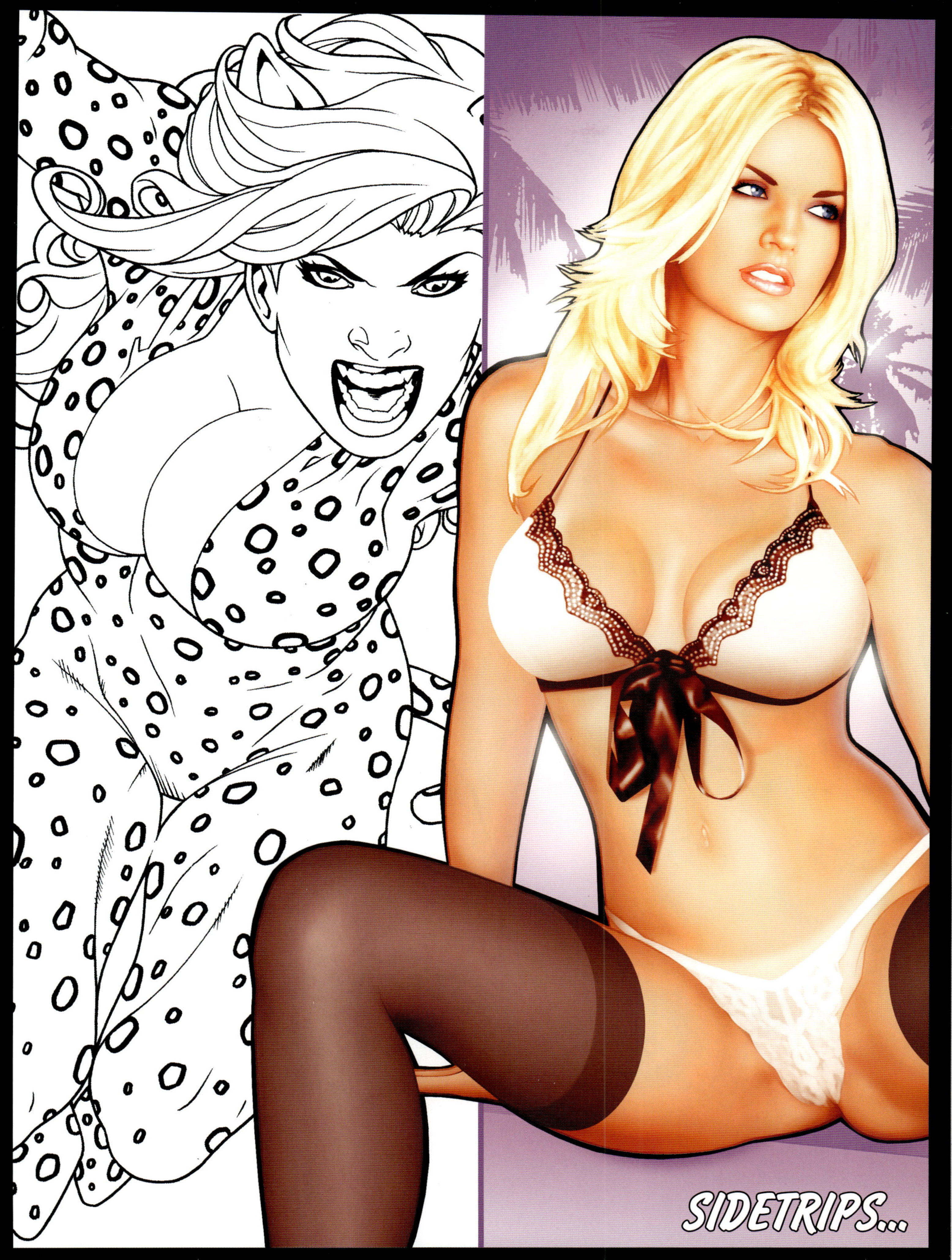
SIDETRIPS...

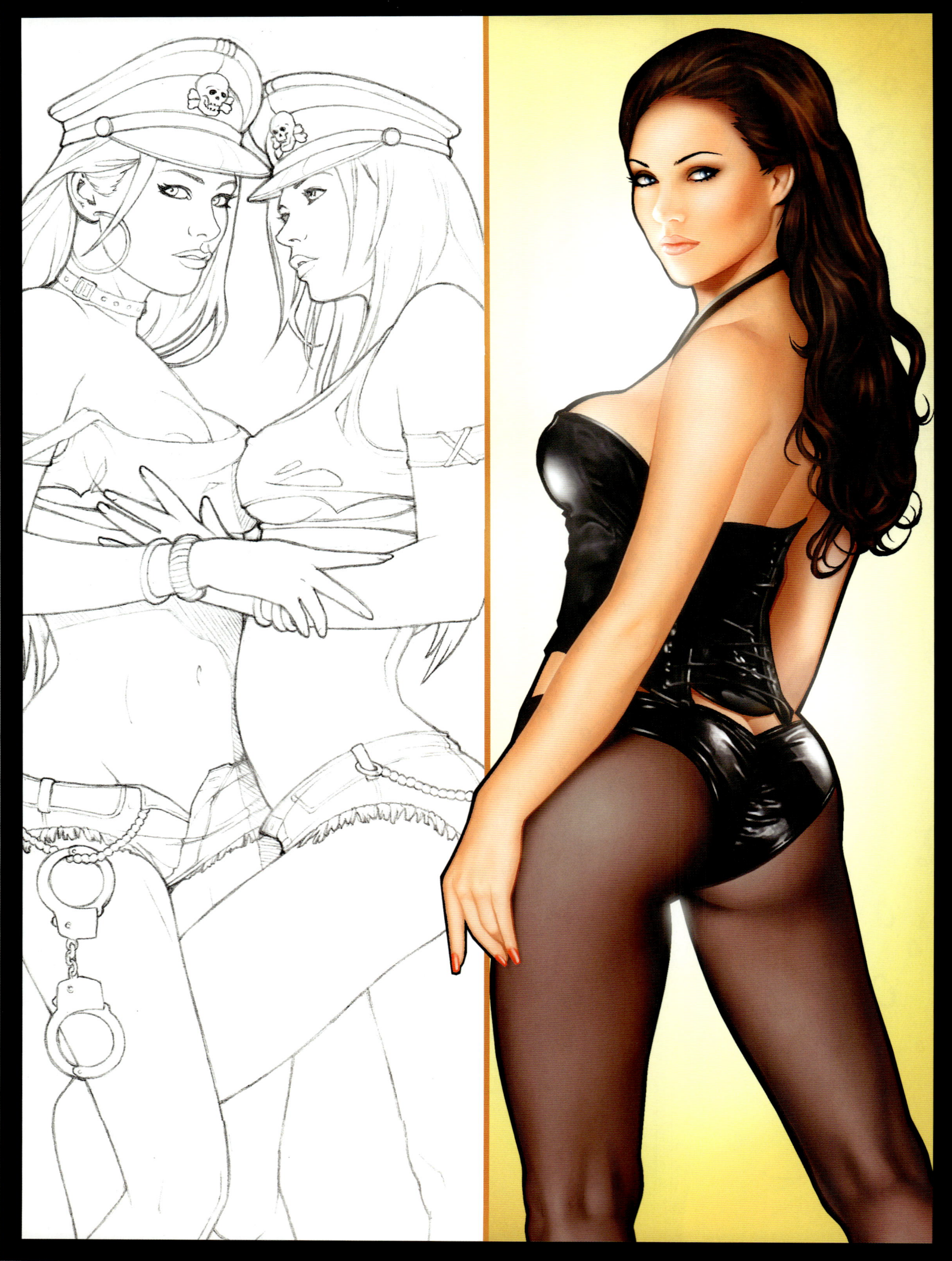

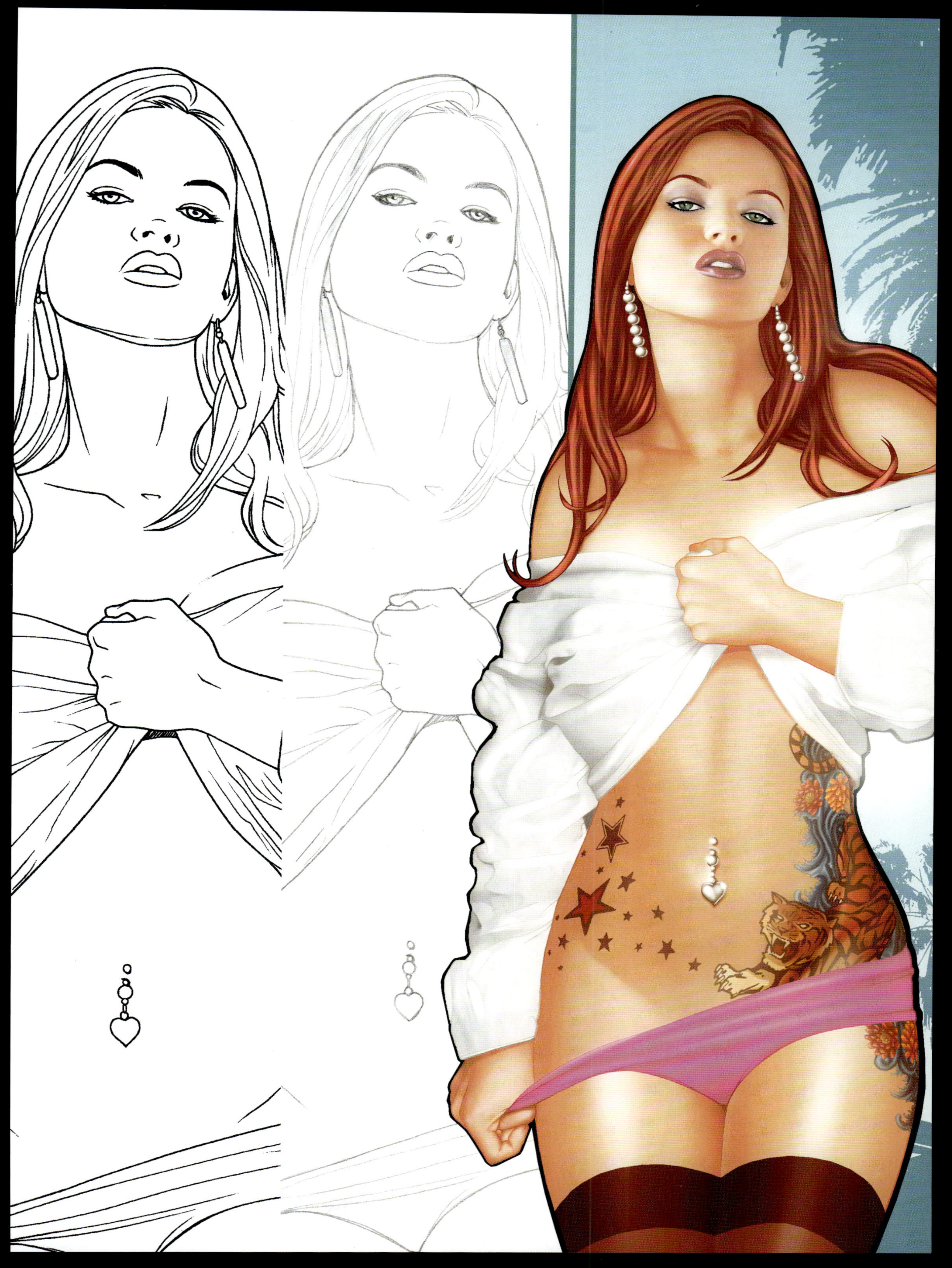

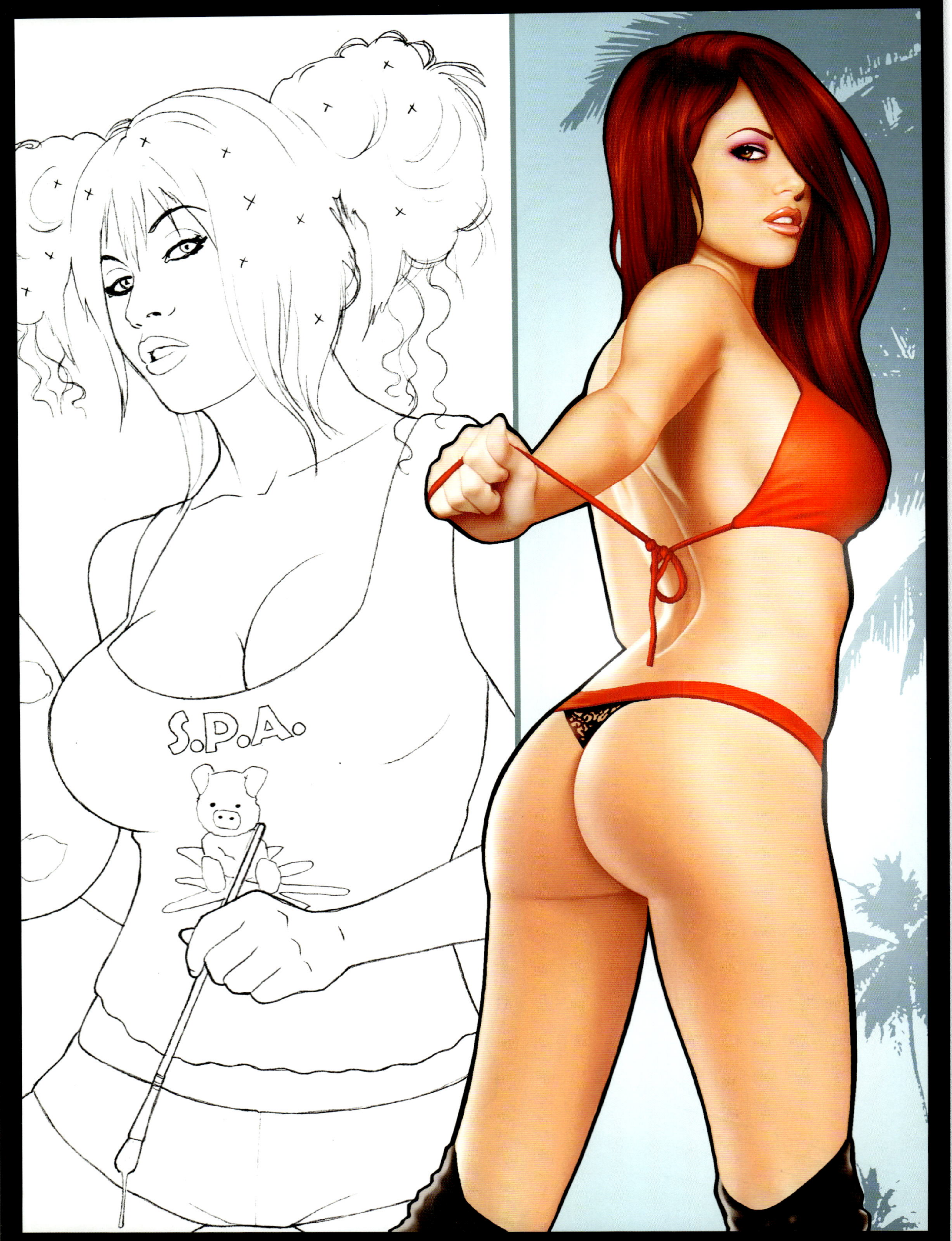
S.P.A.

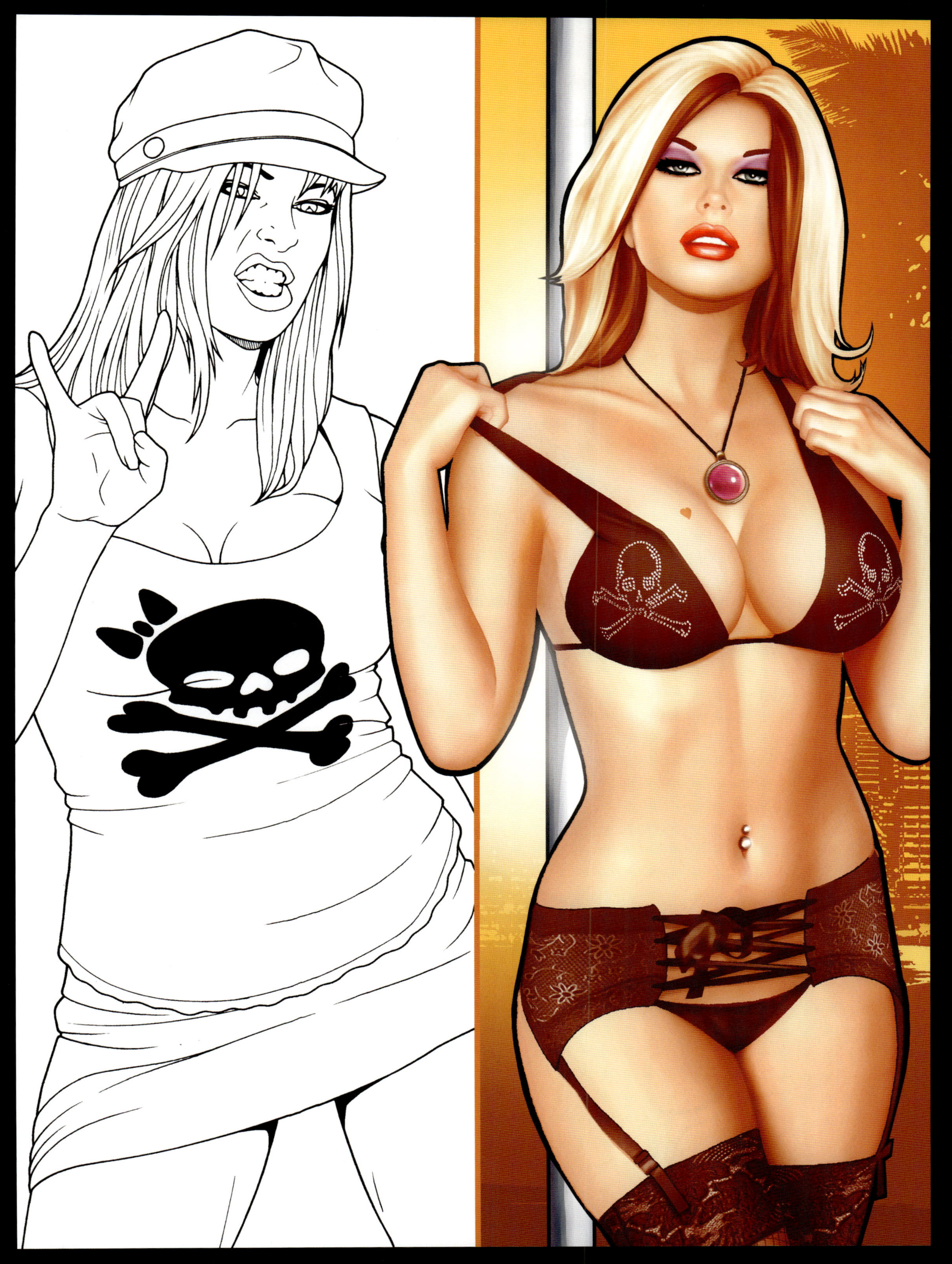

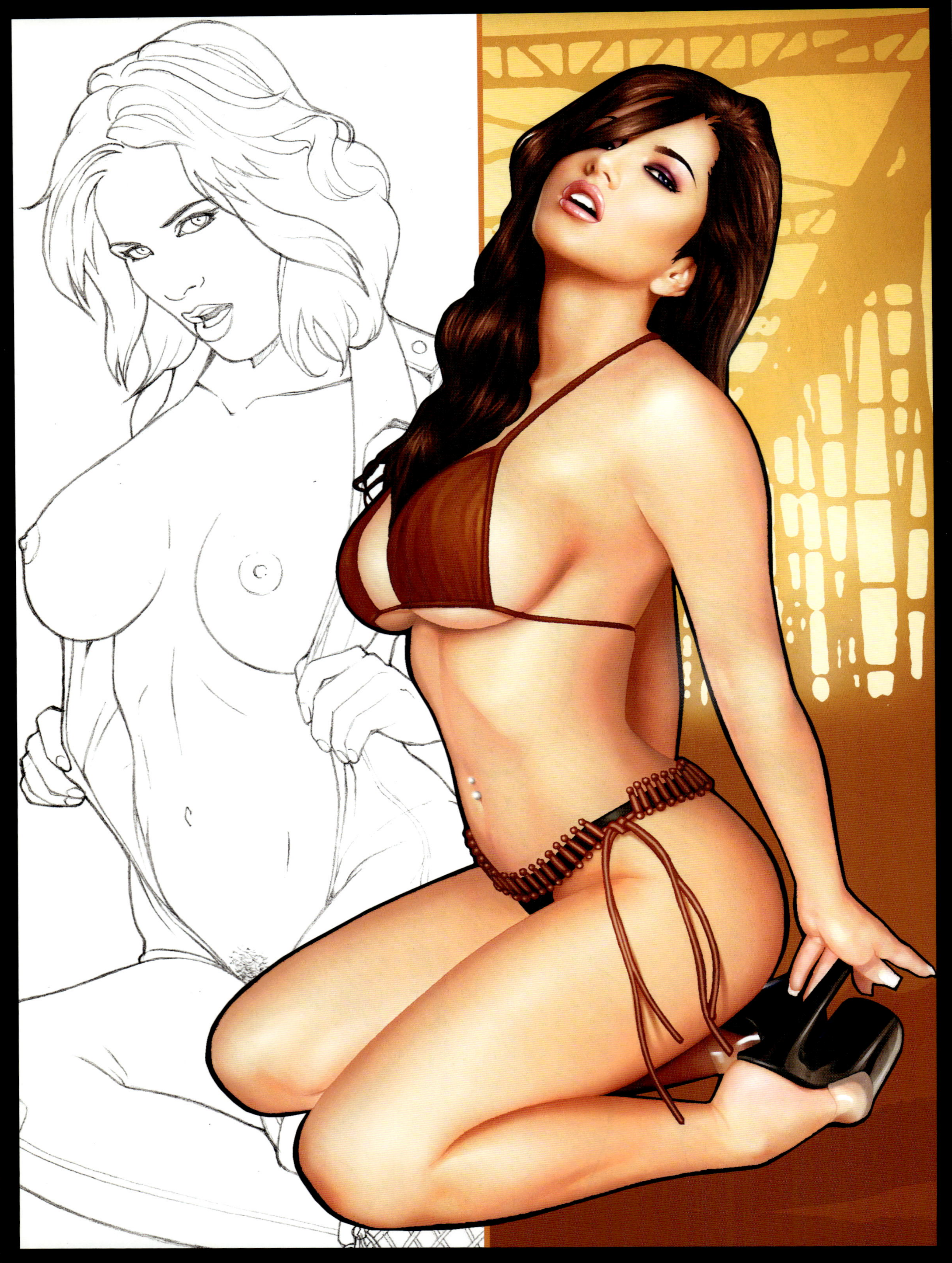

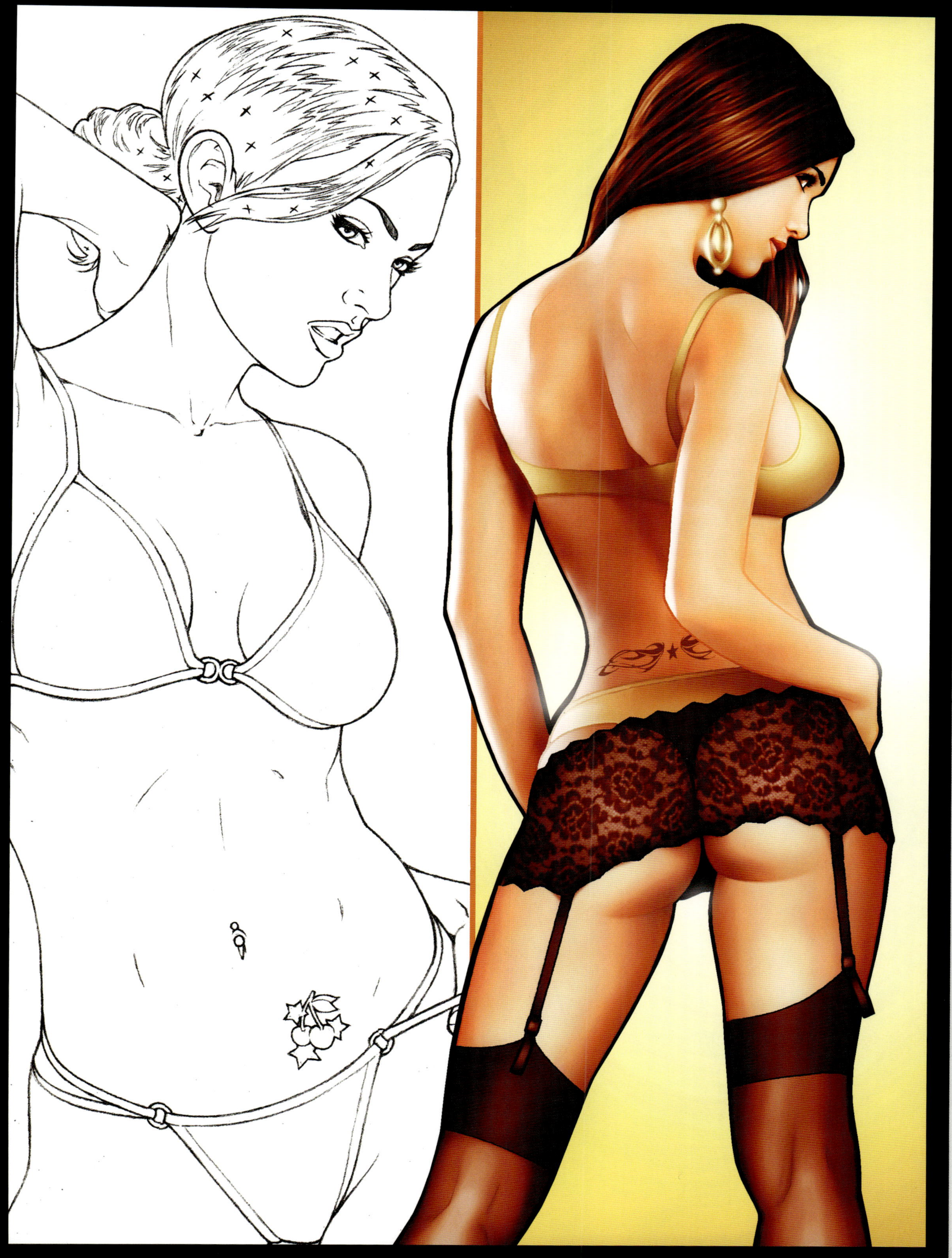

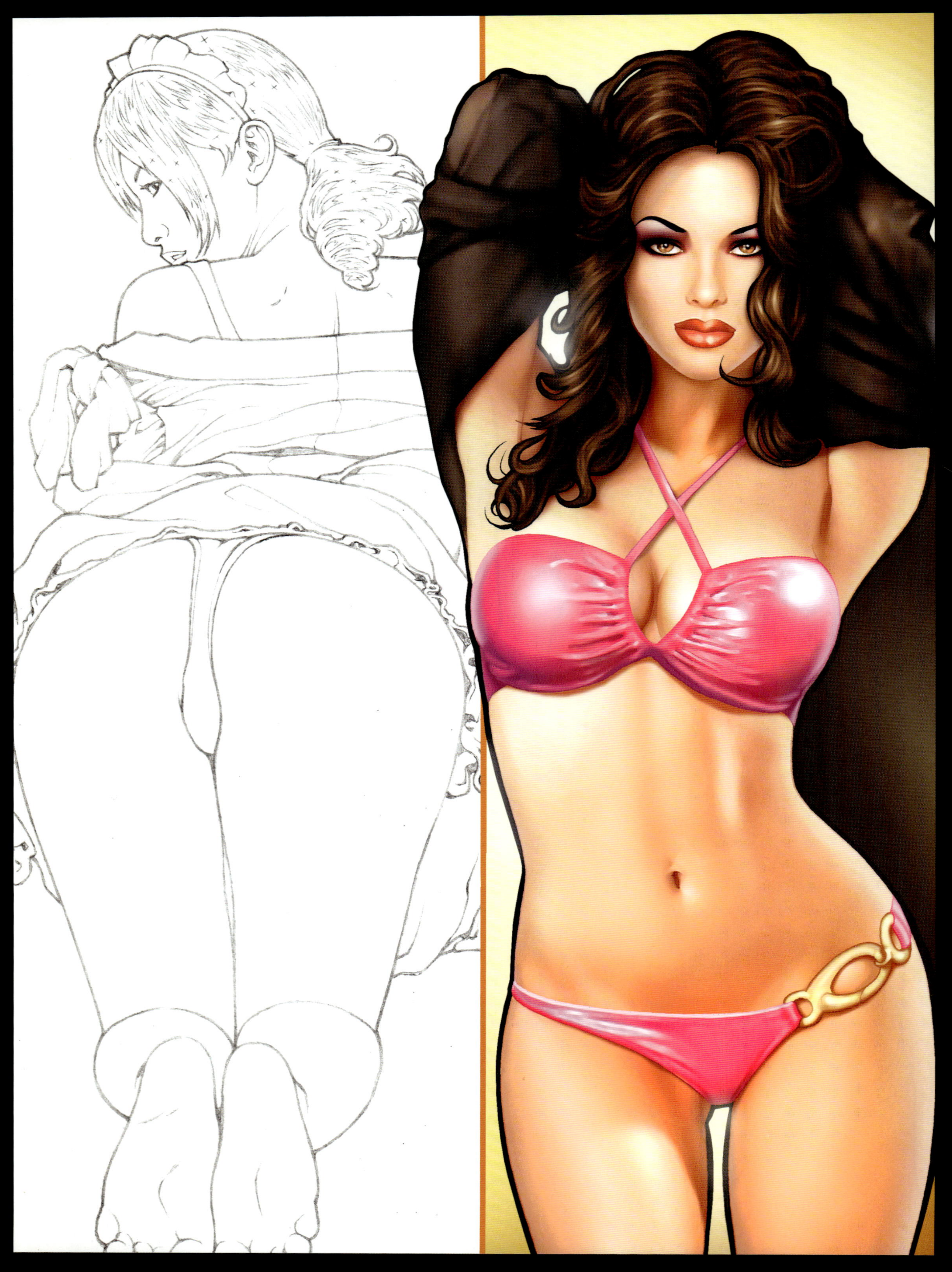

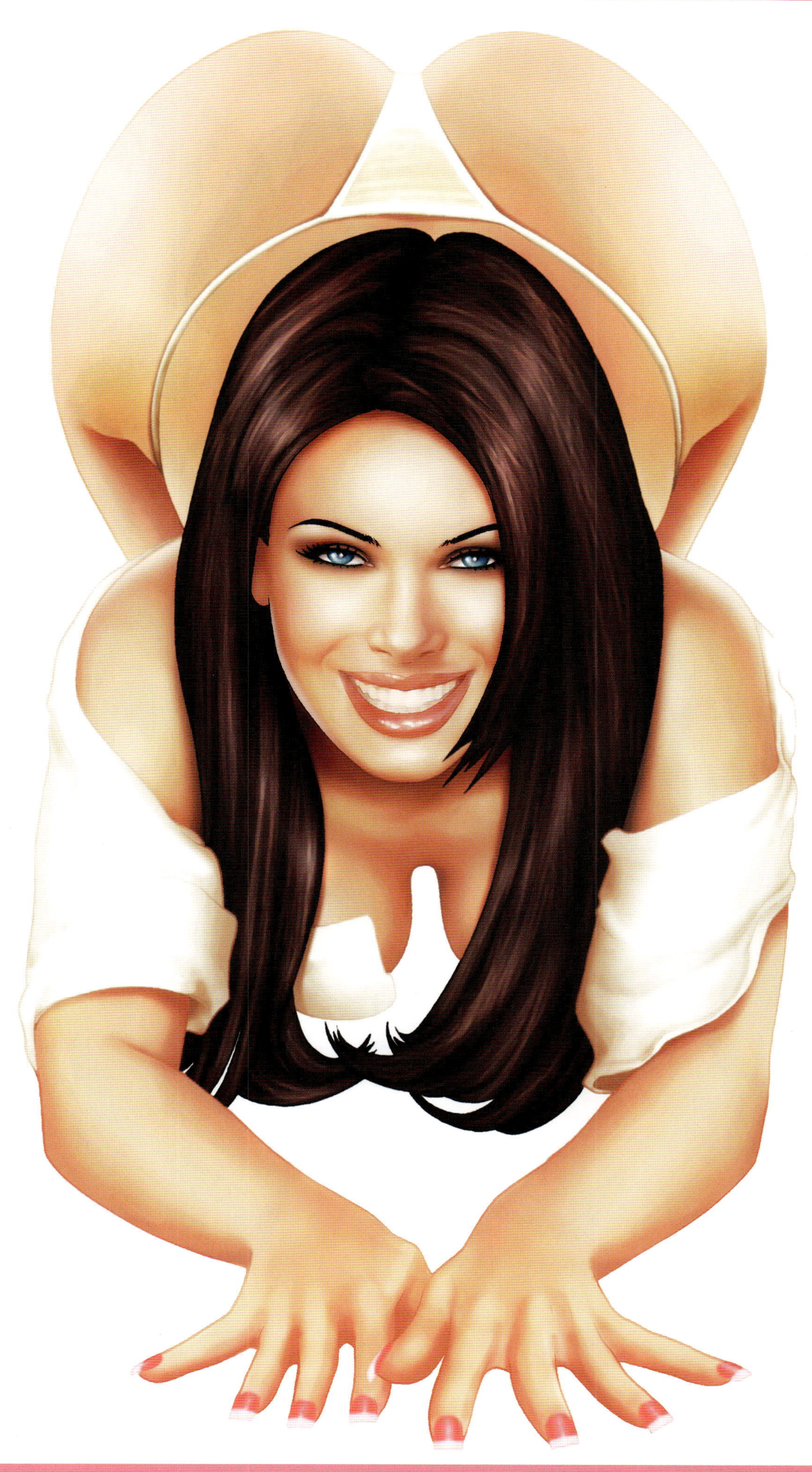

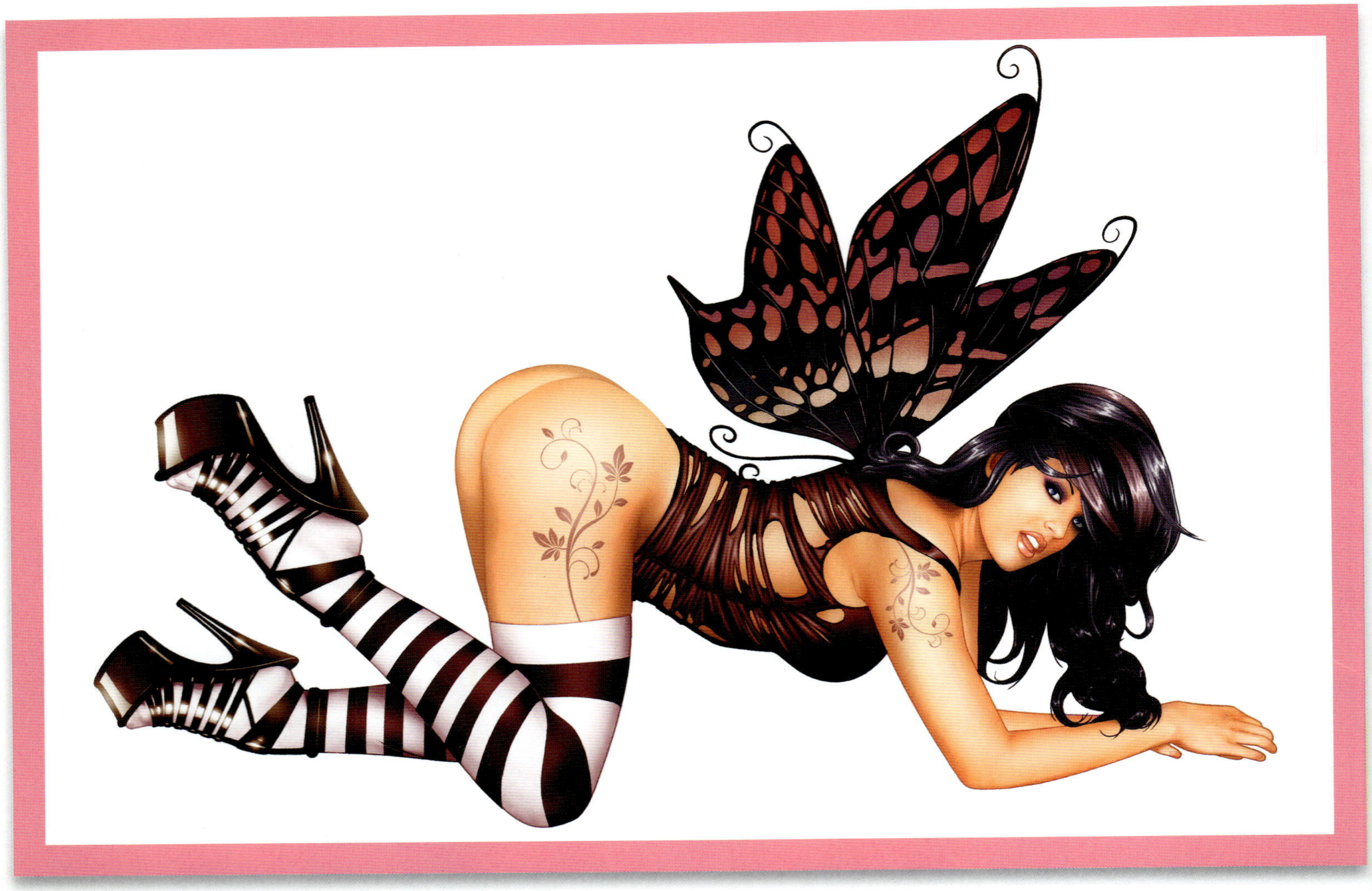

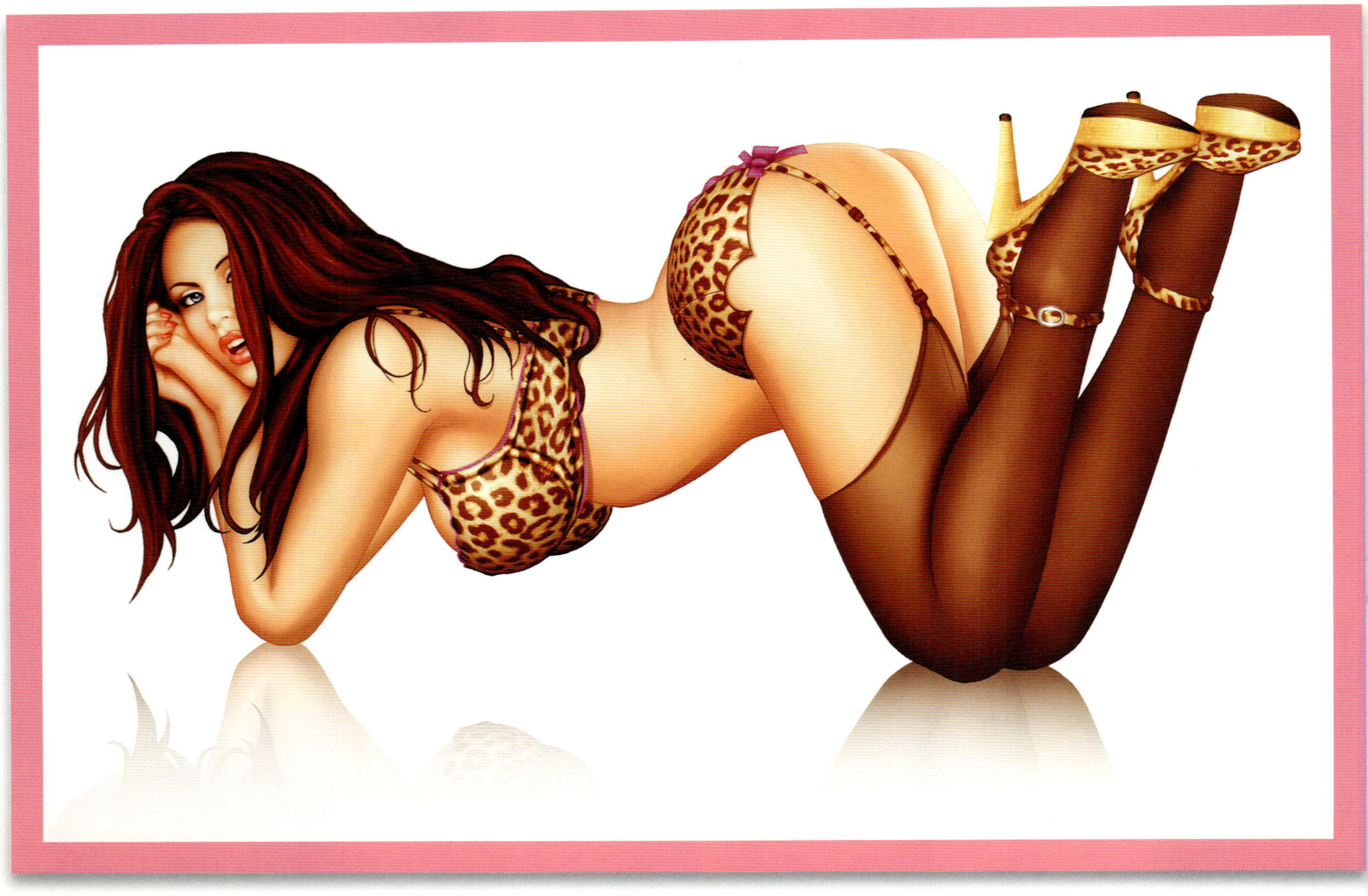

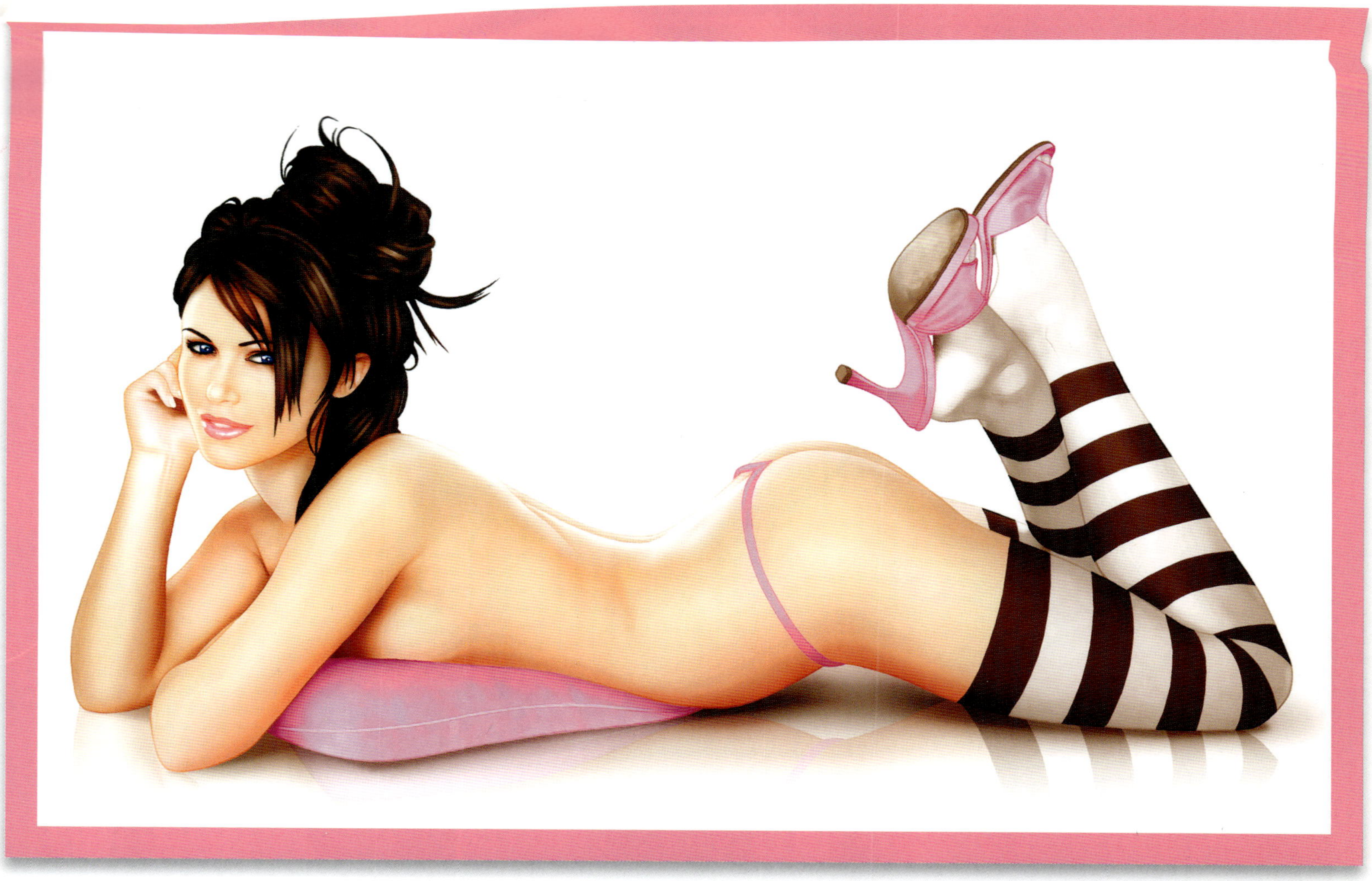

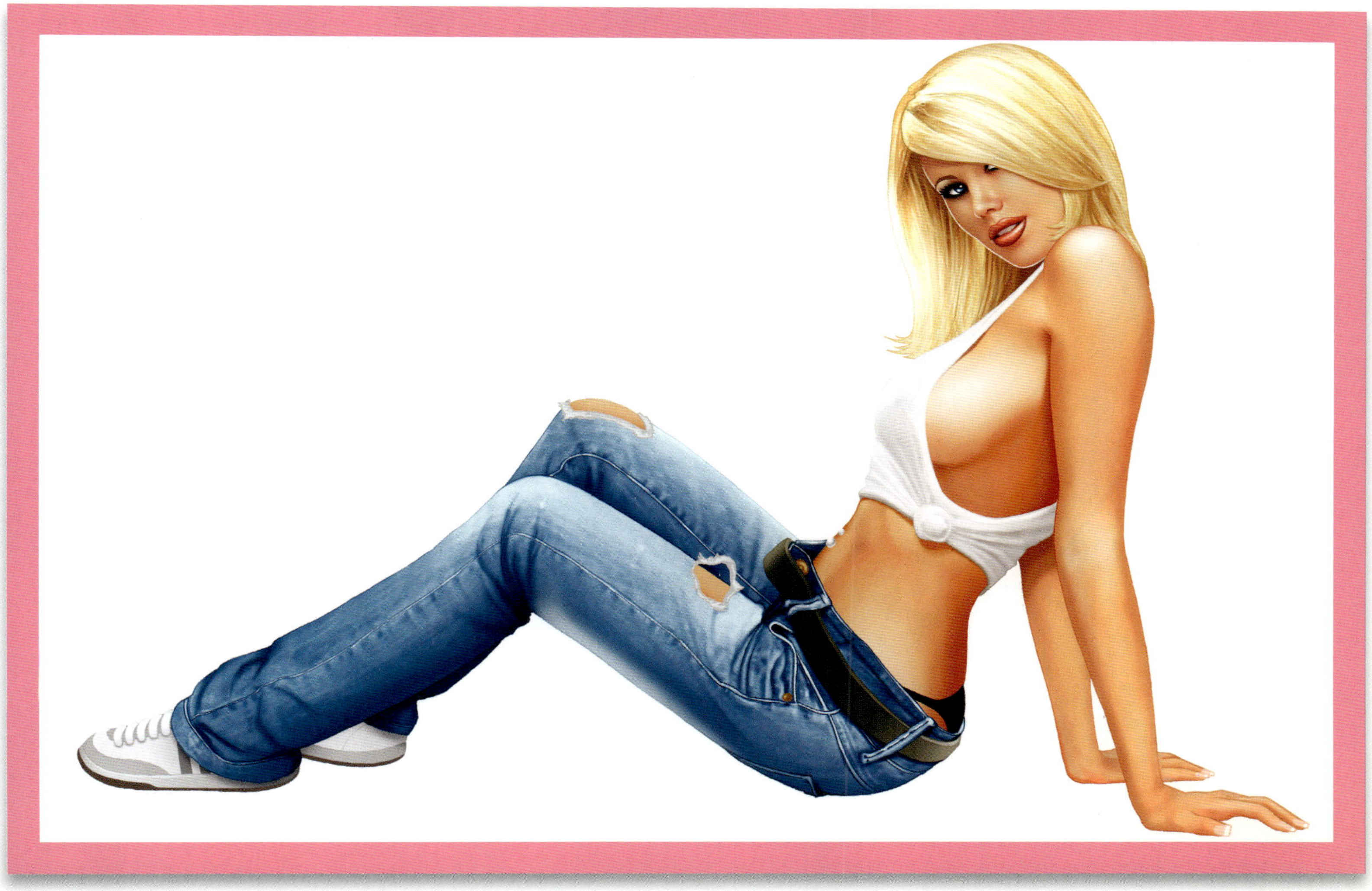

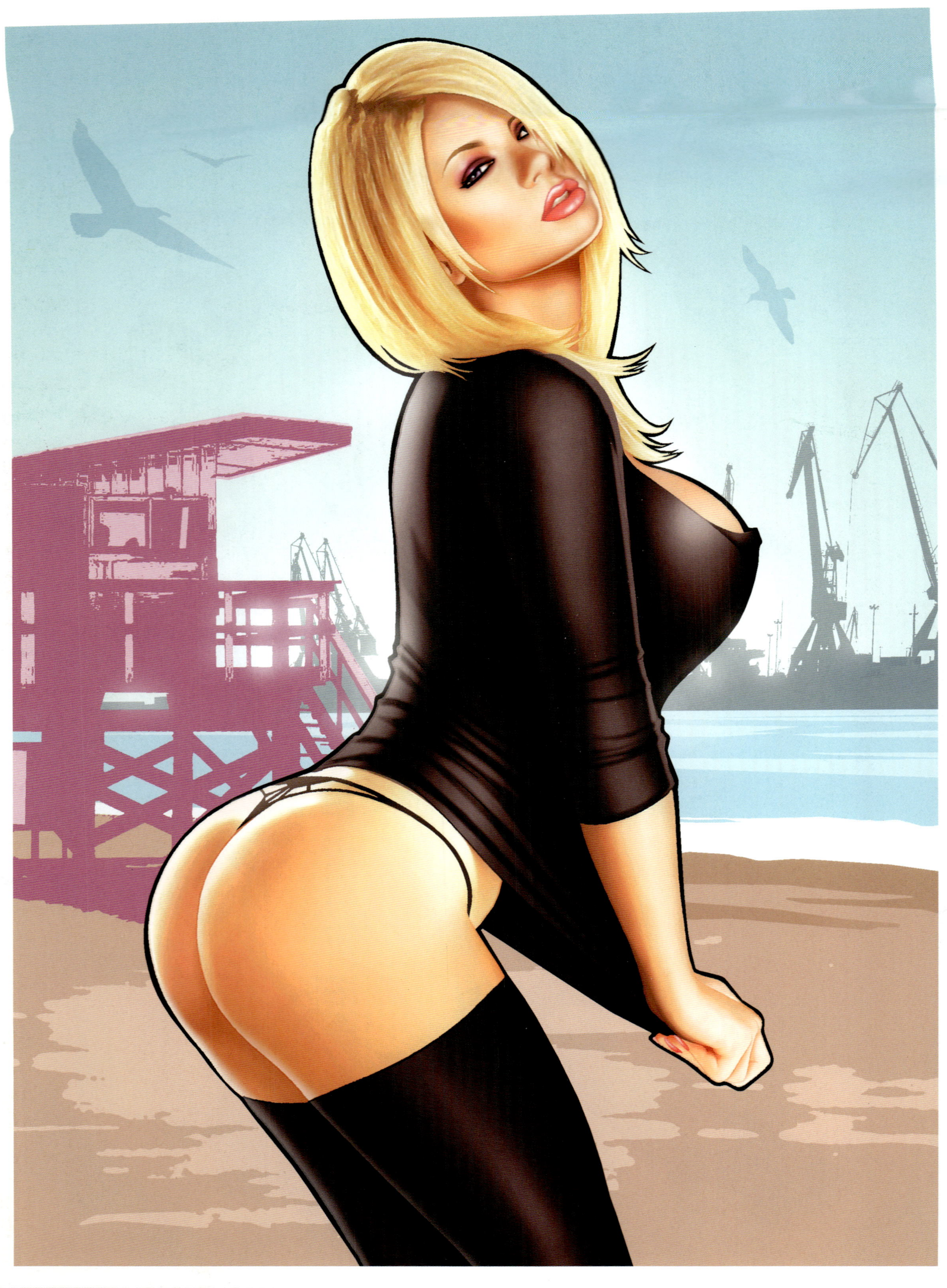

Ah Erika...I hated when she left but I loved to watch her walk away! Wish you were there - José!